PART 1: FOUNDATIONS OF INVESTING

CHAPTER 1: INTRODUCTION TO INVESTING

Why Invest? Understanding Risk and Reward

Investing is one of the most effective ways to build wealth over time, but it requires a solid understanding of the risks and rewards involved. At its core, investing involves putting your money into assets—such as stocks, bonds, or real estate—with the expectation that they will grow in value over time. Unlike saving, which focuses on preserving money, investing aims to make your money work for you by increasing its value.

Why should you invest?

There are several reasons why investing is important:

1. **Beat Inflation**: Over time, inflation erodes the purchasing power of money. Simply saving cash in a bank account with low interest may not keep up with inflation, meaning your money loses value in real terms. Investing offers the potential to grow your wealth at a rate that outpaces inflation.
2. **Achieve Financial Goals**: Whether you're saving for retirement, buying a house, or funding a child's education, investing can help you reach your long-term financial goals faster by offering higher potential returns compared to savings accounts or certificates of deposit (CDs).

3. **Build Wealth**: The ultimate goal of investing is to increase your wealth. By putting your money into appreciating assets, you give it the opportunity to grow. Historically, the stock market has offered annual returns of 7% to 10% over the long term, which can significantly grow your initial investment.

Risk and Reward: A Balancing Act

All investments come with some degree of risk. Understanding the relationship between risk and reward is key to making smart decisions. The basic principle is that **the higher the potential reward, the higher the risk**. Here are the most common types of risks investors face:

- **Market Risk**: The value of your investments can fluctuate due to changes in market conditions. For example, during a stock market downturn, your portfolio's value may decrease temporarily.
- **Inflation Risk**: While investing can help beat inflation, some low-return investments, like bonds or savings accounts, may not grow fast enough to outpace inflation.
- **Liquidity Risk**: This refers to the risk that you won't be able to easily convert an asset into cash without affecting its price.

To mitigate these risks, investors typically diversify their portfolios—investing in a mix of asset types, such as stocks, bonds, and real estate. Diversification spreads out risk, so if one asset class underperforms, others may perform better, helping to protect your overall returns.

Time Horizon: The Key to Managing Risk

Your **time horizon**—the length of time you expect to hold an investment before needing to access your funds—plays a critical role in shaping your investment strategy.

1. **Short-term investing (less than 5 years)**: If you have a short time horizon, your focus should be on minimizing

risk. Investments like bonds or money market funds are often preferred since they offer more stability and less volatility than stocks. However, the potential returns are generally lower.
2. **Long-term investing (more than 5 years):** If you're investing for the long term, you can afford to take on more risk, as you have more time to recover from potential losses. Stocks and real estate tend to offer higher returns over the long run, despite being more volatile in the short term.

In general, the longer your time horizon, the more risk you can take, because the ups and downs of the market tend to smooth out over time.

The Power of Compounding

One of the greatest advantages of long-term investing is the power of **compounding**. Compounding occurs when the returns you earn on an investment start generating their own returns. Essentially, you earn returns on both your original investment and the profits that investment generates.

For example, if you invest $1,000 at a 7% annual return, after one year you'll have $1,070. In the second year, you'll earn 7% on $1,070, not just the original $1,000. Over time, this snowball effect can significantly grow your investment.

Let's illustrate the power of compounding over the long term:
- After 10 years, that same $1,000 investment would grow to about $1,967.
- After 20 years, it would be worth around $3,870.
- After 30 years, it would grow to about $7,612.

The key takeaway is that **the earlier you start investing, the more time you give your money to grow** through compounding. This is why financial experts often advise starting early, even with small amounts.

In summary, investing is a powerful tool to grow your wealth and achieve financial goals, but it requires a balance of understanding risk and reward, matching investments to your time horizon, and taking advantage of the power of compounding. As we proceed through the rest of the book, we'll explore various investment types and strategies to help you make informed decisions based on your unique financial situation.

Year	Initial Investment ($1,000)	Accumulated Return	Total Investment Value
1	$1,000	$70	$1,070
5	$1,000	$402	$1,402
10	$1,000	$967	$1,967
15	$1,000	$1,487	$2,487
20	$1,000	$2,870	$3,870
25	$1,000	$4,439	$5,439
30	$1,000	$6,612	$7,612

Table 1: The Power of Compounding with an Initial Investment of $1,000 at 7% Annual Return

Moving ahead through the rest of the book, we will examine some investment types and strategies that will provide you with greater insight about your specific needs and your capability.

CHAPTER 2: FINANCIAL MARKETS OVERVIEW

Investing effectively requires a solid understanding of the various financial markets where assets are bought and sold. These markets act as platforms where investors trade different types of securities, including stocks, bonds, and commodities. In this chapter, we'll provide a brief overview of the key markets and the financial instruments that play a central role in investing.

Stock Market

The **stock market** is one of the most well-known and widely used financial markets. It's where shares of publicly traded companies are bought and sold. When you buy a stock, you are purchasing partial ownership in a company, making you a shareholder. As a shareholder, you may benefit from dividends (a portion of the company's profits) and capital appreciation (an increase in the stock's value).

Key features of the stock market:

- **Stock Exchanges**: Stocks are primarily traded on exchanges, such as the New York Stock Exchange (NYSE) and NASDAQ. These exchanges provide a regulated platform for investors to buy and sell shares.
- **Public vs. Private Companies**: Only publicly traded companies are listed on stock exchanges, meaning that their shares are available for the public to purchase. Private companies do not trade on exchanges and are owned by individuals or groups of investors.

Stocks are categorized in several ways:
1. **Common Stocks**: The most common type of stock, giving shareholders voting rights and the potential to receive dividends.
2. **Preferred Stocks**: These give priority in receiving dividends but typically don't have voting rights. They often have a fixed dividend, making them less risky than common stocks.

Bond Market

The **bond market** is where investors buy and sell debt securities, typically issued by governments, municipalities, or corporations. When you buy a bond, you are lending money to the issuer in exchange for regular interest payments (called **coupons**) and the return of your principal at the bond's maturity.

Types of Bonds:
- **Government Bonds**: These are issued by national governments to fund spending. U.S. Treasury bonds, for example, are considered some of the safest investments because they are backed by the government.
- **Corporate Bonds**: Issued by companies to raise capital, corporate bonds tend to offer higher returns than government bonds but carry more risk, as the issuer's ability to repay depends on the company's financial health.
- **Municipal Bonds**: These are issued by local governments or municipalities to fund public projects, like building schools or infrastructure. They can offer tax advantages, as the interest earned is often exempt from federal taxes.

How Bonds Work:
- Bonds have a set maturity date, at which point the principal amount (the face value of the bond) is returned to the investor.
- The risk of a bond is measured by its **credit rating**, which is

provided by rating agencies. Higher-rated bonds (like AAA) are considered less risky, while lower-rated bonds (like BB or junk bonds) carry more risk but may offer higher yields.

Commodities Market

The **commodities market** is where raw materials such as gold, oil, natural gas, and agricultural products like wheat and coffee are traded. Commodities are physical goods that investors can buy and sell, and their prices are driven by supply and demand in the global market.

Types of Commodities:

1. **Energy Commodities**: These include oil, natural gas, and coal. Energy prices are influenced by geopolitical events, supply constraints, and changes in technology.
2. **Precious Metals**: Gold, silver, and platinum are popular investment choices in times of economic uncertainty, as they are considered safe-haven assets.
3. **Agricultural Commodities**: Corn, soybeans, coffee, and cotton are examples of agricultural commodities. Their prices can fluctuate based on weather patterns, trade policies, and global demand.

Futures Contracts:

Commodities are often traded through **futures contracts**, which are agreements to buy or sell a specific quantity of a commodity at a predetermined price at a future date. Futures can be used for both speculation and hedging purposes. For example, airlines may use futures contracts to lock in fuel prices, protecting themselves against price spikes.

Key Financial Instruments

1. **Stocks**: Represent ownership in a company, providing potential for capital gains and dividends. They are traded on stock exchanges.
2. **Bonds**: Debt securities that pay regular interest and return the principal at maturity. They are considered

lower risk compared to stocks, especially government bonds.
3. **Commodities**: Physical goods like oil, gold, and agricultural products. They are often traded via futures contracts, offering opportunities for speculation and hedging.
4. **Mutual Funds**: Pooled investment vehicles that allow individuals to invest in a diversified portfolio of stocks, bonds, or other assets. They are professionally managed and provide easy diversification.
5. **Exchange-Traded Funds (ETFs)**: Similar to mutual funds, ETFs hold a diversified portfolio of assets but are traded on stock exchanges like individual stocks. They offer the benefits of diversification and liquidity with typically lower fees.

In summary, understanding the basics of the stock, bond, and commodities markets, as well as the key financial instruments used in these markets, is crucial for making informed investment decisions. Each market offers different risk and return profiles, allowing investors to build diversified portfolios that match their financial goals and risk tolerance.

In the next chapter, we will explore different types of investment strategies, helping you align your goals with the right approach to maximize returns and manage risk effectively.

CHAPTER 3: ECONOMIC INDICATORS AND THEIR IMPACT

Investing isn't just about understanding financial markets and instruments; it's also about understanding how the broader economy influences those markets. Key economic indicators—such as inflation, interest rates, and Gross Domestic Product (GDP)—affect the performance of investments across all asset classes. In this chapter, we'll explore these major economic indicators and how they shape investment decisions.

Inflation

Inflation refers to the increase in the general price level of goods and services in an economy over time. When inflation rises, each unit of currency buys fewer goods and services, effectively reducing purchasing power.

How Inflation Affects Investments:

- **Stocks**: Inflation can hurt stock prices by reducing consumers' purchasing power, which can lead to lower corporate earnings. However, companies with pricing power or those in certain sectors, like energy and commodities, can often pass higher costs onto consumers, benefiting from inflation.
- **Bonds**: Inflation is typically bad news for bondholders.

Bonds pay a fixed interest, and when inflation rises, the real value of these interest payments declines. This is why rising inflation tends to push bond prices down, as investors demand higher yields to compensate for the loss in purchasing power.
- **Commodities**: Commodities, such as oil and gold, tend to perform well in inflationary environments because their prices typically rise with inflation. Investors often use commodities as a hedge against inflation.

Measuring Inflation:
Inflation is usually measured by the **Consumer Price Index (CPI)**, which tracks the average change in prices paid by consumers for goods and services over time. Central banks, like the Federal Reserve, monitor inflation closely and often adjust monetary policies to keep it in check.

Interest Rates

Interest rates represent the cost of borrowing money and are one of the most powerful economic tools central banks use to regulate the economy. Central banks, such as the Federal Reserve in the U.S. or the European Central Bank, set benchmark interest rates to influence economic activity.

How Interest Rates Affect Investments:
- **Stocks**: Lower interest rates are generally good for stocks. When rates are low, borrowing is cheaper, encouraging businesses to invest and consumers to spend, driving corporate profits. In contrast, higher interest rates increase the cost of borrowing, slowing down economic growth and putting downward pressure on stock prices.
- **Bonds**: Bonds have an inverse relationship with interest rates. When interest rates rise, existing bonds with lower yields become less attractive, causing their prices to drop. Conversely, when rates fall, bond prices rise as their yields become more attractive.
- **Real Estate**: Real estate investments are also sensitive to

interest rates. Lower interest rates reduce mortgage costs, making property more affordable and increasing demand. Rising rates, however, tend to slow down the housing market by making borrowing more expensive.

Measuring Interest Rates:
The most closely watched interest rates are those set by central banks, like the **Federal Funds Rate** in the U.S. These rates influence everything from consumer loans to corporate bonds. Investors monitor interest rate changes closely because they can signal shifts in economic policy and impact market performance.

Gross Domestic Product (GDP)

Gross Domestic Product (GDP) measures the total value of all goods and services produced within a country during a specific period. It is the most widely used indicator of a country's economic health. A growing GDP signals a healthy economy, while declining GDP may signal economic trouble.

How GDP Affects Investments:

- **Stocks**: A strong GDP growth rate generally leads to higher corporate earnings, boosting stock prices. Investors see robust economic growth as a sign that companies will increase their sales and profits, which in turn raises stock values. Conversely, when GDP growth slows or contracts, it often leads to lower earnings and stock market declines.
- **Bonds**: When GDP is growing strongly, central banks may raise interest rates to prevent the economy from overheating, which can negatively affect bond prices. In contrast, during periods of slow GDP growth or recession, central banks may lower interest rates to stimulate the economy, boosting bond prices.
- **Commodities**: Commodity demand is closely tied to GDP growth. For example, in a growing economy, demand for energy and raw materials tends to rise, driving commodity prices higher. However, during economic slowdowns, demand for commodities may drop, pushing prices lower.

Measuring GDP:

GDP is reported quarterly, and two main methods are used to track it: **nominal GDP** (not adjusted for inflation) and **real GDP** (adjusted for inflation). Investors pay close attention to GDP reports to gauge the overall health of the economy and anticipate how markets may react.

How the Economy Influences Investments

The performance of financial markets is deeply interconnected with the overall state of the economy. Here's how economic trends influence various asset classes:

- **Recessions**: During economic downturns, businesses earn less, unemployment rises, and consumer spending falls, leading to declines in stock prices. Bonds, especially government bonds, often perform better during recessions as investors seek safer assets.
- **Economic Booms**: In periods of economic expansion, company earnings typically rise, pushing up stock prices. Interest rates may also rise to prevent overheating, which can hurt bond prices but may drive up the yields of new bond issues.
- **Global Factors**: Global economic trends, such as international trade tensions, geopolitical events, and commodity price shocks, can have ripple effects on financial markets. For example, an oil supply disruption can lead to higher energy prices, affecting industries that rely on fuel.

In conclusion, understanding key economic indicators such as inflation, interest rates, and GDP is crucial for making informed investment decisions. These indicators provide valuable insights into the current and future health of the economy, helping investors navigate market fluctuations and capitalize on opportunities. As you continue reading, we'll delve deeper into various asset classes and strategies, keeping these economic principles in mind.

PART 2: KEY INVESTMENT TYPES

CHAPTER 4: STOCK MARKET BASICS

The stock market offers a range of opportunities for investors to grow their wealth, but navigating it requires a basic understanding of the different types of stocks and how to analyze them effectively. In this chapter, we'll introduce the various types of stocks available to investors and the fundamental tools used to analyze and evaluate stocks.

Types of Stocks

Stocks represent ownership in a company, and when you purchase stock, you become a shareholder. There are different types of stocks, each with its own characteristics and benefits. Understanding these differences is crucial for building a diversified portfolio.

1. **Common Stock**
   - **Ownership and Voting Rights**: Most investors hold common stock, which grants ownership in a company and voting rights on corporate matters, such as electing board members or approving mergers.
   - **Dividends**: Common stockholders may receive dividends—payments made from a company's profits—but dividends are not guaranteed. Companies may choose to reinvest profits instead of distributing them to shareholders.
   - **Capital Gains**: The primary way common stockholders make money is through capital gains, which occur when the price of the stock rises above the purchase

price, allowing the investor to sell it for a profit.

2. **Preferred Stock**
   o **Dividend Priority**: Preferred stockholders receive dividends before common stockholders, and these dividends are usually fixed. Preferred stock is often compared to bonds because of its predictable income stream.
   o **No Voting Rights**: Unlike common stockholders, preferred shareholders typically do not have voting rights.
   o **Less Volatility**: Preferred stocks are less volatile than common stocks, making them more attractive to conservative investors. However, they also offer less potential for price appreciation.

3. **Growth Stocks**
   o **High Growth Potential**: Growth stocks belong to companies that are expected to grow at a faster rate than the overall market. These companies often reinvest profits to fuel further expansion, meaning they may not pay dividends.
   o **Higher Risk, Higher Reward**: Growth stocks can offer significant capital appreciation, but they also come with higher risks, as the company's success depends on its ability to continue expanding.

4. **Value Stocks**
   o **Undervalued Companies**: Value stocks represent companies that are considered undervalued by the market. These stocks trade at a lower price relative to their earnings or other fundamentals, providing opportunities for investors to buy them at a discount.

- **Stable but Slower Growth**: Value stocks tend to belong to more mature companies with stable earnings, making them attractive to investors seeking steady returns with lower risk.

5. **Dividend Stocks**
   - **Steady Income**: Dividend stocks are issued by companies that pay out a portion of their earnings regularly. These stocks are appealing to investors looking for a reliable income stream, especially retirees.
   - **Less Volatility**: Dividend-paying companies are often well-established and financially stable, which makes these stocks less volatile compared to growth stocks.

How to Analyze Stocks

Investors use two primary methods to analyze stocks: **fundamental analysis** and **technical analysis**. Both methods help investors make informed decisions about which stocks to buy, hold, or sell.

1. **Fundamental Analysis**
   - **Overview**: Fundamental analysis focuses on evaluating a company's financial health and growth potential. It involves studying financial statements, economic conditions, and industry trends to determine the stock's intrinsic value. The goal is to identify stocks that are undervalued or have strong long-term growth potential.

2. **Key Metrics**:
   - **Earnings per Share (EPS)**: EPS is a measure of a company's profitability and is calculated by dividing net income by the number of outstanding shares. A rising EPS often indicates a company is growing its profits.

- **Price-to-Earnings Ratio (P/E)**: The P/E ratio compares a company's stock price to its earnings per share. A high P/E ratio suggests that investors expect high future growth, while a low P/E ratio may indicate that a stock is undervalued.
- **Price-to-Book Ratio (P/B)**: This ratio compares a company's stock price to its book value (assets minus liabilities). A low P/B ratio may indicate that the stock is undervalued.
- **Dividend Yield**: This metric shows the percentage of a stock's price that a company pays out in dividends annually. A high dividend yield can be attractive to income-seeking investors, but it's important to check if the company's dividend payments are sustainable.

3. **Technical Analysis**
   - **Overview**: Unlike fundamental analysis, technical analysis focuses on stock price movements and trading volumes. Investors who use technical analysis study charts and patterns to predict future price movements.

4. **Key Tools**:
   - **Moving Averages**: A moving average smooths out price data to identify trends. The **50-day** and **200-day moving averages** are popular indicators used to gauge the overall direction of a stock's price.
   - **Relative Strength Index (RSI)**: RSI measures the speed and change of price movements and is used to identify overbought or oversold conditions. An RSI above 70 suggests that a stock may be overbought, while an RSI below 30 indicates it may be oversold.
   - **Support and Resistance Levels**: These are price points where a stock tends to face buying or selling pressure. **Support levels** indicate where buyers typically step

in, while **resistance levels** mark where sellers often start selling. Identifying these levels can help investors decide when to buy or sell.

Combining Both Approaches

Many investors use a combination of both fundamental and technical analysis to make well-rounded decisions. For example, an investor may use fundamental analysis to identify a stock with strong earnings potential and then use technical analysis to find an ideal entry point.

In summary, understanding the types of stocks and how to analyze them is essential for building a successful stock portfolio. Whether you focus on common or preferred stocks, growth or value stocks, or dividend stocks, knowing how to evaluate them through fundamental and technical analysis will help you make informed decisions. As we move forward, we'll dive deeper into different asset classes and explore strategies for managing risk and maximizing returns.

CHAPTER 5: BONDS AND FIXED INCOME

Bonds and other fixed-income securities are essential components of many investment portfolios, providing steady income and diversification away from riskier assets like stocks. In this chapter, we will cover the basics of government and corporate bonds, as well as key concepts like yield and duration, to help you understand how bonds work and how they fit into an investment strategy.

Understanding Government and Corporate Bonds

A bond is essentially a loan made by an investor to a borrower (such as a government or a corporation). In return for the loan, the borrower agrees to pay interest over a specified period and to return the principal (or face value) of the bond when it matures. Bonds are a key component of the fixed-income market because they provide predictable interest payments.

Government Bonds

- **Definition**: Government bonds are issued by national, state, or municipal governments to finance public projects and ongoing operations. These bonds are considered lower-risk investments because they are backed by the issuing government's ability to raise taxes or print money.
- **Types of Government Bonds**:
    1. **Treasury Bonds**: Issued by the U.S. government, Treasury bonds (T-bonds) have long maturities, typically ranging from 10 to 30 years, and are

considered one of the safest investments in the world. They offer lower yields because of this safety.
2. **Municipal Bonds**: Issued by local governments, municipal bonds (or "munis") often come with tax advantages, such as tax-exempt interest at the federal or state level. They are attractive to investors in higher tax brackets seeking tax-free income.
3. **International Bonds**: These are issued by foreign governments and can offer higher yields but also come with additional risks, such as currency fluctuations and political instability.

Corporate Bonds

- **Definition**: Corporate bonds are issued by companies to raise capital for expansion, acquisitions, or other business needs. These bonds tend to offer higher yields than government bonds but come with a higher level of risk, since the ability of the company to repay depends on its financial health.
- **Categories of Corporate Bonds**:
    1. **Investment-Grade Bonds**: These are bonds issued by companies with strong credit ratings (typically rated BBB or higher by credit rating agencies). They carry lower risk and offer lower yields.
    2. **High-Yield Bonds**: Also known as "junk bonds," these are issued by companies with lower credit ratings (BB or below) and come with higher default risk. Investors are compensated for this risk with higher yields.

Key Bond Features

- **Maturity Date**: Bonds have a set maturity date, which is when the issuer repays the face value of the bond. Bonds can have short (less than 3 years), medium (3-10 years), or long-term (10+ years) maturities.

- **Coupon Rate**: The coupon rate is the interest paid by the bond issuer, expressed as a percentage of the face value. This payment is typically made semi-annually or annually.
- **Face Value**: The face value (or par value) is the amount that will be returned to the bondholder when the bond matures. Most bonds have a face value of $1,000, but this can vary.

Yield and Duration

To assess the potential return and risk of bonds, investors need to understand the concepts of **yield** and **duration**.

Yield

Yield refers to the return an investor can expect to earn from a bond. Several types of yields are commonly used in bond analysis:

1. **Current Yield**:
   - This is the annual interest payment divided by the bond's current market price. It gives an idea of the income generated relative to the bond's price.

2. **Formula**:

$$\text{Current Yield} = \frac{\text{Annual Coupon Payment}}{\text{Current Price of Bond}}$$

For example, if a bond has a $1,000 face value, a 5% coupon, and is currently trading at $950, the current yield would be:

$$\text{Current Yield} = \frac{50}{950} \approx 5.26\%$$

- **Yield to Maturity (YTM)**:
   - YTM is a more comprehensive measure of a bond's total return, as it considers both the bond's coupon payments and any gain or loss if the bond is held until

maturity.
- **YTM** assumes that all interest payments are reinvested at the same rate and that the bond is held to maturity. This yield is often used to compare bonds with different coupon rates and prices.

3. **Yield to Call (YTC):**
- Some bonds are callable, meaning the issuer has the right to repay the bond before its maturity date. The **yield to call** measures the return if the bond is called early, often at a premium to its face value.

DURATION

Duration measures a bond's sensitivity to changes in interest rates. The higher the duration, the more sensitive a bond is to interest rate fluctuations. Duration is expressed in years, but it is not the same as the bond's maturity.

- **Modified Duration**: This is an estimate of how much the price of a bond will change in response to a 1% change in interest rates. A bond with a duration of 5 years will lose roughly 5% of its value if interest rates rise by 1%.
- **Why Duration Matters**: Investors need to understand duration because bond prices move inversely to interest rates. When interest rates rise, bond prices fall, and the longer the duration, the greater the price decline.

For example, if you hold a bond with a duration of 6 and interest rates rise by 1%, the bond's price will decrease by approximately 6%. Conversely, if interest rates fall by 1%, the bond's price will increase by 6%.

Key Risks in Bond Investing

- **Interest Rate Risk**: The risk that rising interest rates will cause the price of bonds to fall. Long-term bonds are more sensitive to interest rate changes than short-term bonds.
- **Credit Risk**: The risk that the issuer will default on its payments. Corporate bonds, especially high-yield ones, carry higher credit risk than government bonds.
- **Inflation Risk**: The risk that rising inflation will erode the purchasing power of the bond's fixed interest payments. Inflation-protected bonds, such as **Treasury Inflation-Protected Securities (TIPS)**, can help mitigate this risk.

- **Call Risk**: The risk that a bond will be called, or redeemed by the issuer, before maturity. This often happens when interest rates decline, as companies can issue new debt at lower rates.

In summary, bonds and fixed-income securities provide a reliable stream of income and help diversify investment portfolios. Understanding the types of bonds, how to evaluate yields, and the importance of duration allows investors to make more informed decisions. As we progress, we will explore how bonds fit into a broader portfolio and how to balance them with other asset classes for a well-rounded investment strategy.

CHAPTER 6: MUTUAL FUNDS AND ETFS

Mutual funds and exchange-traded funds (ETFs) are popular investment vehicles that allow individuals to pool their money with other investors to access a diversified portfolio of assets. In this chapter, we'll explore how these funds work, their key differences, and the concepts of active versus passive management.

How Funds Work

Both mutual funds and ETFs function by collecting money from multiple investors and using that capital to invest in a diversified pool of assets such as stocks, bonds, or other securities. The main difference between these two types of funds lies in how they are structured and traded.

Mutual Funds

- **Definition**: A mutual fund is a type of investment fund that pools money from multiple investors to purchase a basket of securities. When you invest in a mutual fund, you own a share of the fund, not the underlying assets.
- **How They Trade**: Mutual funds are bought and sold at the fund's **net asset value (NAV)**, which is calculated at the end of each trading day. Investors place orders during the day, but the price is finalized at market close.
- **Minimum Investment**: Many mutual funds require a minimum investment, which could range from a few hundred to several thousand dollars.

Types of Mutual Funds:
1. **Equity Funds**: These invest primarily in stocks and aim to achieve growth. They may focus on specific sectors, company sizes, or geographic regions.
2. **Bond Funds**: These invest in bonds and seek to provide regular income through interest payments, often with lower risk than equity funds.
3. **Balanced Funds**: These hold a mix of stocks and bonds to offer both growth and income while managing risk.
4. **Index Funds**: These aim to replicate the performance of a specific index, such as the S&P 500. They are passively managed (more on this below) and generally have lower fees.

ETFs (Exchange-Traded Funds)

- **Definition**: Like mutual funds, ETFs pool money from multiple investors to buy a basket of securities. However, ETFs are traded on an exchange, like a stock, and their price fluctuates throughout the trading day based on supply and demand.
- **How They Trade**: ETFs are bought and sold in real-time during market hours at a price that can vary from the fund's net asset value (NAV). This makes ETFs more liquid and accessible for investors who want flexibility in their trading.
- **Lower Investment Barrier**: ETFs typically do not have minimum investment requirements, making them accessible to investors with smaller amounts of capital.

Types of ETFs:
1. **Stock ETFs**: These ETFs track a specific stock market index, sector, or country's stock market.
2. **Bond ETFs**: These invest in a basket of bonds and provide fixed income, similar to bond mutual funds.
3. **Commodity ETFs**: These track the price of commodities such as gold, oil, or agricultural products.

4. **Thematic ETFs**: These focus on specific investment themes like technology, renewable energy, or healthcare innovation.

Active vs. Passive Management

One of the key decisions investors face when choosing mutual funds or ETFs is whether to opt for active or passive management. This decision has a significant impact on cost, performance, and investment strategy.

Active Management

- **What It Is**: In an actively managed fund, a portfolio manager or team actively selects and trades securities in an attempt to outperform a market index or benchmark. The manager makes decisions based on research, market forecasts, and their own investment expertise.
- **Pros**:
  - **Potential for Outperformance**: Active managers aim to beat the market by picking high-performing investments or avoiding poorly performing ones.
  - **Flexibility**: Active managers can adjust the portfolio quickly in response to changing market conditions or new opportunities.
- **Cons**:
  - **Higher Fees**: Actively managed funds typically charge higher fees, known as **expense ratios**, to cover the costs of research, trading, and management. These higher fees can eat into returns over time.
  - **Risk of Underperformance**: Despite the goal of outperforming the market, many actively managed funds fail to do so over the long term, especially after accounting for fees.

Passive Management

- **What It Is**: Passive management involves creating a portfolio that mirrors the performance of a market index, such as the S&P 500. Passive funds, such as **index funds** and most **ETFs**, do not aim to beat the market but to match its performance.

- **Pros**:
  - **Lower Fees**: Because there is no need for active decision-making or frequent trading, passive funds have significantly lower fees compared to active funds.
  - **Market Performance**: Passive funds typically match the performance of their benchmark, providing reliable, long-term returns that reflect the overall market's performance.
- **Cons**:
  - **Limited Flexibility**: Passive funds are not designed to respond to market downturns or take advantage of specific investment opportunities. They follow the index, regardless of whether individual securities in the index perform well or poorly.

Key Considerations When Choosing Between Mutual Funds and ETFs

1. **Cost**:
   - ETFs generally have lower expense ratios than mutual funds, especially when comparing passive ETFs to actively managed mutual funds. Additionally, ETFs typically do not have the same fees for buying or selling shares as mutual funds do (e.g., sales loads or redemption fees).
2. **Tax Efficiency**:
   - ETFs tend to be more tax-efficient than mutual funds due to their structure. Mutual funds often trigger capital gains taxes for investors when the fund manager buys or sells securities, while ETFs typically do not because they use an "in-kind" creation and redemption process that limits taxable events.
3. **Trading Flexibility**:
   - Mutual funds are priced at the end of the trading

day, which can be a drawback if you want to react to market movements in real time. ETFs trade like stocks, allowing for real-time buying and selling during market hours.
4. **Investment Strategy**:
    - If you prefer a hands-off, long-term approach that tracks the market, a passively managed index fund or ETF may be ideal. However, if you're looking for opportunities to outperform the market and are willing to pay higher fees for professional management, actively managed mutual funds may be more suitable.

In conclusion, both mutual funds and ETFs offer diversification and access to a range of assets, but they differ in structure, cost, and trading flexibility. The choice between active and passive management depends on your investment goals, risk tolerance, and cost considerations. As you continue building your investment knowledge, understanding these differences will help you choose the right funds to achieve your financial objectives.

CHAPTER 7: REAL ESTATE INVESTMENT

Real estate is a popular investment choice because it offers the potential for both steady income and long-term appreciation. In this chapter, we'll explore the two primary ways to invest in real estate: **Real Estate Investment Trusts (REITs)** and **direct property ownership**. We'll also discuss the pros and cons of investing in real estate to help you determine whether it fits into your broader investment strategy.

REITs (Real Estate Investment Trusts)

REITs offer a way for investors to gain exposure to real estate without the need to directly buy or manage property. They are companies that own, operate, or finance income-producing real estate across various sectors, such as residential, commercial, or industrial properties.

How REITs Work

- **Ownership**: REITs pool money from multiple investors to buy and manage a portfolio of properties. Investors purchase shares of the REIT, similar to buying shares of a stock.
- **Income Stream**: REITs are required by law to distribute at least 90% of their taxable income to shareholders as dividends, making them an attractive option for income-seeking investors.
- **Types of REITs**:
    1. **Equity REITs**: These own and operate income-generating real estate, such as office buildings,

apartments, or shopping malls. Equity REITs earn money through rent collected from tenants and property appreciation.
2. **Mortgage REITs (mREITs)**: These provide financing for income-producing properties by purchasing or originating mortgages. Mortgage REITs earn income from interest on the loans they hold.
3. **Hybrid REITs**: These invest in both properties and mortgages, combining aspects of equity and mortgage REITs.

Benefits of REITs:

1. **Liquidity**: Unlike direct property ownership, REITs are traded on major stock exchanges, allowing investors to buy and sell shares easily.
2. **Diversification**: REITs provide exposure to a broad portfolio of properties, which helps spread risk across different types of real estate and geographic locations.
3. **Accessibility**: REITs require significantly less capital to invest in compared to purchasing real estate directly, making them accessible to a wider range of investors.
4. **Dividend Income**: The mandatory high dividend payout makes REITs an attractive option for income investors.

Drawbacks of REITs:

1. **Market Volatility**: REITs can be affected by broader stock market volatility, even if the underlying real estate assets are stable.
2. **Tax Efficiency**: Dividends from REITs are generally taxed as ordinary income, which can result in higher taxes compared to long-term capital gains.
3. **Limited Control**: Investors in REITs have no direct say in property management decisions, leaving all operations to the REIT's management team.

Direct Property Ownership

Direct property ownership involves buying and managing physical real estate, whether for personal use or as an investment property. Investors can earn returns through rental income, property value appreciation, or both.

Types of Direct Property Investments:

1. **Residential Real Estate**: This includes single-family homes, multi-family properties, or vacation rentals. Residential properties are often easier for individual investors to manage.
2. **Commercial Real Estate**: This involves office buildings, retail spaces, warehouses, or industrial properties. Commercial properties tend to offer higher rental income but also come with more complex management and greater risks.
3. **Land**: Some investors purchase undeveloped land with the goal of developing it or selling it later at a profit. This can be riskier, as land generates no income and depends entirely on future appreciation.

Benefits of Direct Property Ownership:

1. **Tangible Asset**: Real estate is a physical asset that provides shelter, workspaces, or services, making it inherently valuable.
2. **Steady Income**: Rental properties provide regular income through rent, which can help offset expenses like mortgage payments, maintenance, and property taxes.
3. **Appreciation Potential**: Over time, property values typically increase, especially in desirable locations. This can lead to substantial capital gains when the property is sold.
4. **Tax Advantages**: Real estate investors can take advantage of various tax benefits, including depreciation, mortgage interest deductions, and deferrals of capital gains through strategies like **1031**

exchanges.

Drawbacks of Direct Property Ownership:

1. **High Capital Requirement**: Purchasing real estate often requires a significant upfront investment, including the down payment, closing costs, and renovation expenses.
2. **Illiquidity**: Real estate is not easily sold, and it may take months or even years to sell a property, especially in a slow market.
3. **Management Responsibility**: Owning and managing a rental property involves significant time and effort, from finding tenants to handling maintenance and repairs. Some investors hire property management companies, but this adds to the cost.
4. **Market Risk**: Real estate markets can fluctuate based on economic conditions, interest rates, and local factors, which can affect property values and rental income.

Pros and Cons of Real Estate Investment

Pros:

1. **Diversification**: Real estate offers diversification from traditional assets like stocks and bonds. Real estate often behaves differently from other asset classes, which can reduce overall portfolio risk.
2. **Inflation Hedge**: Real estate is often seen as a hedge against inflation because property values and rents tend to rise with inflation, preserving purchasing power.
3. **Leverage Opportunities**: Investors can use borrowed capital (mortgages) to buy properties, amplifying potential returns. However, this also increases risk if property values decline or rental income falls short.

Cons:

1. **Illiquidity**: Whether through direct ownership or REITs, real estate is less liquid than assets like stocks or bonds. Direct property ownership is especially illiquid,

as selling a property can take considerable time.
2. **High Transaction Costs**: Real estate transactions come with high costs, including agent fees, closing costs, and ongoing maintenance expenses, which can reduce overall returns.
3. **Market Volatility**: While real estate often provides stability, it is not immune to economic downturns. Property values can drop, and rental demand can decrease in times of economic stress, leading to reduced income or losses.

In conclusion, real estate investments, whether through REITs or direct property ownership, offer a unique way to diversify your portfolio and generate income. REITs provide a more accessible, liquid option with less hands-on management, while direct property ownership offers the potential for greater control and long-term wealth building. Both have their benefits and drawbacks, and understanding these factors will help you decide which type of real estate investment best aligns with your goals and risk tolerance.

CHAPTER 8: CRYPTOCURRENCIES AND EMERGING ASSETS

Cryptocurrencies have rapidly emerged as a new asset class, offering both exciting opportunities and significant risks for investors. In this chapter, we will introduce the fundamentals of **Bitcoin** and **altcoins**, and explore the risks, regulations, and potential future of these digital assets.

Introduction to Bitcoin and Altcoins

Bitcoin: The First Cryptocurrency

Bitcoin, introduced in 2009 by an anonymous entity known as **Satoshi Nakamoto**, is the first and most well-known cryptocurrency. It is a decentralized digital currency that allows for peer-to-peer transactions without the need for a central authority, such as a bank or government. Instead, Bitcoin transactions are verified by a network of computers (known as miners) and recorded on a public ledger called the **blockchain**.

Bitcoin's key features:

- **Limited Supply**: There will only ever be 21 million bitcoins, making it a deflationary asset, which some view as a hedge against inflation.
- **Decentralization**: Bitcoin operates on a decentralized

network, meaning no single entity has control over the currency.
- **Security**: Transactions on the Bitcoin network are secured through a process called **proof of work**, which requires miners to solve complex mathematical problems to validate transactions.

Altcoins: Alternatives to Bitcoin

Following Bitcoin's success, thousands of other cryptocurrencies, often referred to as **altcoins**, have been created. These altcoins are digital currencies with different features, use cases, and technologies compared to Bitcoin. Some of the more well-known altcoins include **Ethereum (ETH)**, **Litecoin (LTC)**, and **Ripple (XRP)**. Each altcoin aims to improve on or offer alternatives to Bitcoin's limitations.

- **Ethereum (ETH)**: Ethereum is not only a cryptocurrency but also a decentralized platform that allows developers to create and run smart contracts and decentralized applications (dApps). Ethereum's network enables automated agreements and applications without intermediaries.
- **Litecoin (LTC)**: Litecoin was developed to be the "silver to Bitcoin's gold." It is designed to process transactions faster and with lower fees compared to Bitcoin.
- **Ripple (XRP)**: Ripple is focused on enabling fast, low-cost cross-border payments. Unlike Bitcoin and Ethereum, Ripple is not fully decentralized, as its founders hold a significant portion of the XRP tokens.

Use Cases of Cryptocurrencies

1. **Digital Payments**: Cryptocurrencies like Bitcoin and Litecoin are used for direct payments, allowing users to send money globally without relying on banks or traditional financial systems.
2. **Decentralized Finance (DeFi)**: Platforms like Ethereum have enabled a new ecosystem called **DeFi**, which allows users to lend, borrow, and trade assets without

intermediaries, using blockchain technology.
3. **Store of Value**: Some investors view Bitcoin as a store of value similar to gold, due to its limited supply and decentralized nature.

Risks of Cryptocurrencies

While the potential rewards of investing in cryptocurrencies are significant, so are the risks. Cryptocurrencies are highly speculative, and their value can be extremely volatile. Some of the key risks to consider include:

Volatility

Cryptocurrencies are known for their extreme price fluctuations. Bitcoin, for instance, has experienced rapid rises in value followed by significant crashes. This volatility can create both opportunities for large gains and the risk of substantial losses. Investors should be prepared for extreme price swings.

Regulatory Uncertainty

Cryptocurrency regulation varies significantly by country and is still evolving. Some governments have embraced cryptocurrencies, while others have imposed restrictions or outright bans. Regulatory changes can have a major impact on cryptocurrency prices and the ability to use or trade digital assets.

For example:

- **China** has taken a hardline stance, banning cryptocurrency trading and mining.
- **The United States** is still developing its regulatory framework, with various agencies like the SEC scrutinizing whether certain cryptocurrencies should be classified as securities.

Security and Fraud Risks

While blockchain technology itself is highly secure, the broader cryptocurrency ecosystem is vulnerable to hacking, fraud, and scams. Cryptocurrency exchanges, where digital assets are bought and sold, have been frequent targets of cyberattacks. If an exchange is hacked, investors could lose their funds, as cryptocurrencies are often not insured like traditional bank accounts.

Additionally, the anonymous nature of cryptocurrency transactions has attracted criminals, leading to concerns about money laundering and illegal activities.

Lack of Consumer Protections

Cryptocurrency investments are not typically protected by government-backed insurance programs, such as the **Federal Deposit Insurance Corporation (FDIC)** in the U.S. This means that if a platform holding your cryptocurrency fails or is hacked, there may be no recourse to recover your assets.

Regulation of Cryptocurrencies

Cryptocurrencies operate in a legal gray area in many parts of the world, with governments and regulators seeking to catch up to the rapid innovation in this space. As a result, regulatory frameworks are still being developed and can vary widely by region.

KYC and AML Compliance

Most governments are introducing regulations to combat money laundering and ensure that cryptocurrencies are not used for illegal activities. **Know Your Customer (KYC)** and **Anti-Money Laundering (AML)** regulations require cryptocurrency exchanges to verify the identities of their users. This is a move toward greater transparency but also reduces some of the privacy and decentralization that originally attracted many to cryptocurrencies.

Taxation

Cryptocurrencies are increasingly being recognized as taxable assets. In many countries, including the United States, cryptocurrency transactions are subject to **capital gains tax**, meaning that investors must report any profits made from buying and selling digital currencies. This adds a layer of complexity for investors, as they must track and report every transaction for tax purposes.

Government Bans and Restrictions

In some countries, such as **India** and **China**, governments have considered or implemented bans on cryptocurrency trading and mining. These regulatory changes can have a significant impact on the global cryptocurrency market, often leading to dramatic price shifts.

Is Cryptocurrency a Good Investment?

The decision to invest in cryptocurrencies depends on your risk tolerance and long-term financial goals. While cryptocurrencies offer significant growth potential, they come with equally significant risks.

Pros:

1. **High Growth Potential**: Cryptocurrencies, especially Bitcoin and Ethereum, have delivered outsized returns for early investors. As adoption grows, some believe there is still room for substantial gains.
2. **Diversification**: Adding cryptocurrencies to your portfolio can offer diversification beyond traditional assets like stocks and bonds. Cryptocurrencies tend to behave differently from these assets, providing a potential hedge.
3. **Innovation and Utility**: Blockchain technology and decentralized finance (DeFi) are pushing the boundaries of how financial systems operate. Investors see long-term potential in these technologies.

Cons:

1. **High Risk and Volatility**: Cryptocurrencies are speculative and can experience large price swings in short periods. Many have lost significant value in past

market downturns.
2. **Regulatory Uncertainty**: The future regulatory environment remains unclear, and adverse regulations could negatively impact the cryptocurrency market.
3. **Security Concerns**: Cryptocurrency exchanges and wallets can be vulnerable to hacking, and once assets are stolen, they are often impossible to recover.

In conclusion, cryptocurrencies represent an emerging asset class with high growth potential and significant risks. Bitcoin and altcoins provide new ways to think about currency, payments, and investment, but their volatility, regulatory uncertainty, and security concerns make them a speculative choice. If you choose to invest in cryptocurrencies, ensure they align with your broader financial goals and risk tolerance.

PART 3: INVESTMENT STRATEGIES

CHAPTER 9: VALUE AND GROWTH INVESTING

When building an investment portfolio, one of the key decisions an investor faces is choosing between value and growth stocks. These two approaches represent distinct strategies for selecting stocks, each with its own philosophy, characteristics, and potential for returns. In this chapter, we will explore the fundamentals of value and growth investing and examine real-world examples to illustrate how each strategy works.

Value Investing: Buying Undervalued Companies

Value investing is the strategy of buying stocks that appear to be trading for less than their intrinsic or true value. The goal is to identify companies whose stock prices do not fully reflect their underlying fundamentals, creating an opportunity for investors to buy at a "discount" and benefit from future price appreciation when the market corrects the mispricing.

Key Characteristics of Value Stocks:

1. Low Price-to-Earnings (P/E) Ratio: Value stocks often have a low P/E ratio, indicating that they are relatively cheap compared to their earnings.
2. High Dividend Yields: Value companies tend to be mature and established businesses that may offer dividends, providing income to investors.
3. Stable Business Models: Value stocks are typically in

industries with steady cash flows, such as utilities, consumer staples, and financials.
4. Undervalued by the Market: These companies may be temporarily out of favor with the market due to short-term challenges, but their long-term prospects remain strong.

Example of Value Investing:

- Warren Buffett: Perhaps the most famous value investor, Warren Buffett has built his career by identifying undervalued companies. Through his company Berkshire Hathaway, Buffett has invested in well-known value stocks like Coca-Cola and American Express. Despite being household names, these companies were purchased when the market undervalued their potential.
- Case Study: Bank of America: After the 2008 financial crisis, Bank of America's stock price plummeted, and many investors abandoned the financial sector. However, value investors like Buffett saw long-term potential, recognizing that the bank's fundamentals would recover over time. Those who invested at the time reaped significant returns as the stock price rebounded in the following years.

Advantages of Value Investing:

1. Lower Risk: Because value stocks are typically priced lower relative to their earnings or book value, they may offer a margin of safety, reducing the risk of a major loss.
2. Income Generation: Many value stocks offer dividends, providing income even if the stock price does not appreciate rapidly.
3. Outperformance During Market Downturns: Historically, value stocks tend to perform better during periods of market volatility or economic uncertainty, as their prices are less inflated.

Disadvantages of Value Investing:

1. Slow Growth: Value stocks may take longer to realize their potential, requiring patience from investors.
2. Value Traps: Sometimes, a stock appears undervalued for a reason—such as declining business prospects or poor management. These "value traps" can lead to poor long-term performance if the company does not recover.

Growth Investing: Capturing Future Potential

Growth investing focuses on companies that are expected to grow their earnings and revenues at an above-average rate compared to the market. Investors in growth stocks are willing to pay a premium for these companies, believing that their high growth potential will lead to significant returns in the future. Growth stocks typically do not pay dividends, as companies reinvest earnings back into their businesses to fuel expansion.

Key Characteristics of Growth Stocks:

1. High P/E Ratio: Growth stocks often have high P/E ratios, as investors are willing to pay more for future earnings potential.
2. No or Low Dividends: Growth companies typically reinvest their profits into expansion rather than paying dividends to shareholders.
3. Disruptive or Innovative: Growth companies are often leaders in their industries, offering new products, services, or technologies that disrupt existing markets.
4. High Volatility: Growth stocks can experience more significant price swings, as their valuations are more dependent on future expectations than current fundamentals.

Example of Growth Investing:

- Amazon (AMZN): For many years, Amazon operated with slim profits, choosing to reinvest nearly all its earnings into expanding its infrastructure, developing new products, and acquiring businesses. Despite its low profitability, investors recognized Amazon's enormous growth potential, pushing its stock price higher. Over time, Amazon has evolved into one of the world's most valuable companies, rewarding growth investors with substantial returns.

- Case Study: Tesla (TSLA): Tesla is another classic example of a growth stock. For years, the electric vehicle maker faced skepticism due to its high valuations and inconsistent profitability. However, growth investors believed in Tesla's potential to revolutionize the auto industry. As demand for electric vehicles increased, Tesla's stock price soared, making early growth investors significant profits.

Advantages of Growth Investing:

1. High Potential Returns: Growth stocks offer the possibility of outsized returns if the company's earnings and revenues grow as expected.
2. Leadership in New Markets: Growth companies are often pioneers in fast-growing industries like technology, healthcare, and clean energy, offering investors exposure to innovative sectors.
3. Capital Appreciation: Investors in growth stocks seek capital appreciation, as these companies prioritize reinvestment over dividends.

Disadvantages of Growth Investing:

1. Higher Risk: Growth stocks are often more volatile and risky, as their high valuations depend on continued rapid growth. If a company fails to meet expectations, its stock price can drop sharply.
2. Overvaluation: Growth stocks can become overvalued if investors push prices too high in anticipation of future growth. This can lead to price corrections when growth slows.
3. No Dividends: Growth stocks typically do not offer dividend income, so investors rely solely on price

appreciation for returns.

Real-World Comparison of Value vs. Growth Strategies

- Coca-Cola (Value) vs. Tesla (Growth):
    - Coca-Cola is a classic value stock, offering stable earnings, strong brand recognition, and consistent dividends. Investors buy Coca-Cola for its reliable returns and lower risk.
    - Tesla, on the other hand, is a high-growth company. Investors are betting on Tesla's ability to dominate the electric vehicle market and revolutionize transportation, accepting greater risk for potentially higher rewards.
- Apple (AAPL): Interestingly, Apple has evolved from being considered a growth stock to being viewed as a value stock. Initially, investors flocked to Apple for its innovation and rapid growth in the tech sector. Today, Apple has become a more mature company, offering dividends and steady cash flow, appealing to value investors as well.

Choosing Between Value and Growth Investing

The choice between value and growth investing ultimately comes down to your personal investment goals, time horizon, and risk tolerance.

- For Conservative, Long-Term Investors: Value stocks may be more suitable due to their lower volatility and focus on steady returns.
- For Aggressive, Risk-Tolerant Investors: Growth stocks can offer higher potential rewards, but they come with greater risk and volatility. Investors with a longer time horizon who can weather short-term fluctuations may benefit from a growth strategy.

Many investors also choose to blend the two strategies, investing in both value and growth stocks to create a more balanced portfolio. This approach can provide the potential for high returns from growth stocks while also offering the stability and income generation of value stocks.

In conclusion, both value and growth investing have their merits and risks. Value investing offers a disciplined approach to finding undervalued companies with the potential for steady, long-term returns. Growth investing focuses on identifying companies with high earnings potential that can lead to significant capital appreciation. A clear understanding of these strategies and their differences can help you make informed decisions about which approach aligns with your financial objectives and risk tolerance.

PART 3: INVESTMENT STRATEGIES

CHAPTER 10: INCOME INVESTING

Income investing focuses on generating a steady stream of income from investments, primarily through **dividend stocks** and **bonds**. This approach is especially appealing for retirees or those seeking to supplement their income without relying solely on capital appreciation. In this chapter, we will explore the fundamentals of income investing, including the benefits and risks, and provide guidance on building a portfolio for passive income.

Dividend Stocks

Dividend stocks are shares of companies that return a portion of their earnings to shareholders in the form of dividends. These companies are typically well-established, with stable earnings and a commitment to returning value to investors.

Key Features of Dividend Stocks:

1. **Regular Income**: Dividend stocks provide a predictable income stream, often distributed quarterly, making them attractive for those seeking cash flow.
2. **Compounding Growth**: Reinvesting dividends can enhance total returns through compound growth. Many investors choose to reinvest dividends to purchase more shares, benefiting from the power of compounding over time.
3. **Lower Volatility**: Dividend-paying stocks tend to be less volatile than non-dividend-paying stocks, as they often belong to more stable companies with consistent cash

flows.

Examples of Dividend Stocks:

- **Coca-Cola (KO)**: Known for its strong brand and global presence, Coca-Cola has a long history of paying and increasing dividends, making it a popular choice among income investors.
- **Johnson & Johnson (JNJ)**: With a diversified portfolio of healthcare products, Johnson & Johnson has consistently paid dividends for decades and is considered a reliable income stock.

Evaluating Dividend Stocks:

When selecting dividend stocks, consider the following metrics:

- **Dividend Yield**: This is the annual dividend payment divided by the stock price. A higher yield indicates a more substantial income return.
- **Dividend Growth Rate**: Look for companies that have a history of increasing their dividends over time. This can indicate financial health and a commitment to returning value to shareholders.
- **Payout Ratio**: This ratio measures the percentage of earnings paid out as dividends. A lower payout ratio suggests that the company retains enough earnings to sustain its operations and continue paying dividends.

Bonds

Bonds are fixed-income securities that represent a loan from the investor to a borrower, typically a corporation or government. In exchange for lending money, the investor receives regular interest payments (coupons) and the return of the principal at maturity.

Types of Bonds:

1. **Government Bonds**: Issued by national governments, these bonds are generally considered low-risk. Examples include U.S. Treasury bonds and municipal bonds.

2. **Corporate Bonds**: Issued by companies, these bonds usually offer higher yields than government bonds but come with increased risk. The creditworthiness of the issuing company can impact the bond's yield.
3. **High-Yield Bonds**: Also known as junk bonds, these are issued by companies with lower credit ratings and therefore offer higher interest rates to compensate for increased risk.

Evaluating Bonds:

When considering bonds for an income portfolio, pay attention to:

- **Yield to Maturity (YTM)**: This metric reflects the total return expected if the bond is held until maturity, considering both interest payments and any capital gains or losses.
- **Credit Rating**: Assess the bond's credit rating, typically provided by agencies like Moody's and Standard & Poor's. Higher-rated bonds are considered safer but usually offer lower yields.
- **Duration**: This measures a bond's sensitivity to interest rate changes. Bonds with longer durations are more sensitive to interest rate fluctuations, impacting their market value.

Building a Portfolio for Passive Income

Creating a well-diversified income portfolio involves combining dividend stocks and bonds to balance risk and income generation.

Steps to Build an Income Portfolio:

1. **Determine Income Goals**: Assess how much income you need from your investments to meet your financial objectives. This could be a specific dollar amount or a percentage of your total investment portfolio.
2. **Assess Risk Tolerance**: Understand your risk tolerance to determine the appropriate mix of dividend stocks and bonds. If you prefer lower risk, you might allocate a

higher percentage to bonds.
3. **Diversify Across Sectors and Types**:
   - **Dividend Stocks**: Invest in various sectors (e.g., consumer staples, utilities, healthcare) to spread risk. Consider a mix of high-yield and dividend growth stocks.
   - **Bonds**: Diversify among government and corporate bonds, and consider including bonds with varying maturities to balance interest rate risk.
4. **Rebalance Regularly**: Over time, the value of your investments may shift, impacting your income distribution. Regularly review and rebalance your portfolio to ensure it aligns with your income goals and risk tolerance.
5. **Consider Dividend Reinvestment Plans (DRIPs)**: Many companies offer DRIPs, allowing investors to automatically reinvest dividends into additional shares. This can enhance compounding effects and long-term growth.

Advantages of Income Investing:

1. **Steady Cash Flow**: Income investments provide regular payments, which can be particularly beneficial for retirees or those seeking consistent income.
2. **Lower Volatility**: Income-generating investments, particularly bonds, can be less volatile compared to growth-focused stocks, providing stability during market downturns.
3. **Tax Advantages**: Certain income investments, such as municipal bonds, may offer tax benefits, making them attractive to investors in higher tax brackets.

Disadvantages of Income Investing:

1. **Interest Rate Risk**: Bond prices tend to fall when interest rates rise, potentially leading to capital losses if bonds are sold before maturity.

2. **Inflation Risk**: Income from dividends and bonds may not keep pace with inflation, eroding purchasing power over time.
3. **Limited Growth Potential**: While income investments provide stability, they may not offer the same growth potential as equities, which can lead to lower overall returns in the long term.

In conclusion, income investing through dividend stocks and bonds can be an effective strategy for generating passive income while maintaining a balanced portfolio. By understanding the characteristics of these investments and following a disciplined approach to building your income portfolio, you can achieve your financial goals while enjoying the benefits of regular income. Whether you are seeking to supplement your retirement income or build wealth over time, a well-structured income investment strategy can provide the financial security you desire.

CHAPTER 12: ALTERNATIVE INVESTMENT STRATEGIES

While traditional investments like stocks and bonds are the foundation of most portfolios, many investors seek to diversify further by exploring **alternative investments**. These assets, including **hedge funds**, **private equity**, and **commodities**, can provide unique opportunities for growth, income, and risk management. However, they also come with higher levels of complexity and risk. In this chapter, we'll explore the basics of these alternative strategies, their potential benefits, and the associated risks.

Hedge Funds

Hedge funds are pooled investment vehicles managed by professional portfolio managers who employ a wide range of strategies to generate high returns. Unlike mutual funds, hedge funds often aim for **absolute returns** (positive returns regardless of market conditions) and have more flexibility in the assets they can invest in, including derivatives, currencies, and even distressed assets.

Key Features of Hedge Funds:

1. **Flexible Investment Strategies**: Hedge funds can use various strategies, such as long-short equity (betting

on rising and falling stocks), global macro (making bets based on global economic trends), and arbitrage (exploiting price inefficiencies).
2. **Leverage**: Hedge funds often use borrowed money to amplify their positions, which can lead to higher returns but also increases risk.
3. **Limited Liquidity**: Hedge funds typically require investors to lock up their capital for a certain period (e.g., one year or more), making them less liquid than other investments.
4. **High Fees**: Hedge funds generally charge a management fee (typically 2% of assets under management) and a performance fee (often 20% of any profits made).

Benefits of Hedge Funds:

- **Diversification**: Hedge funds offer exposure to a wide variety of asset classes and investment strategies, which can reduce portfolio risk.
- **Potential for High Returns**: Some hedge funds have delivered outsized returns by taking advantage of market inefficiencies or utilizing sophisticated strategies.

Risks of Hedge Funds:

- **High Risk and Volatility**: The use of leverage and complex strategies can lead to significant losses if the fund's bets go wrong.
- **Lack of Transparency**: Hedge funds are less regulated than mutual funds, so investors may not always have full insight into the fund's holdings or strategies.
- **Illiquidity**: The lock-up period can make it difficult to access your money if needed in the short term.

Private Equity

Private equity involves investing directly in private companies or taking public companies private through buyouts. Private equity firms typically buy underperforming companies, restructure them, and aim to sell them at a profit after a few years. This strategy requires a long-term investment horizon but can yield substantial returns.

Types of Private Equity:

1. **Venture Capital**: Investing in early-stage startups with high growth potential but also high risk.
2. **Buyouts**: Acquiring established companies, often using significant leverage, to improve their operations and eventually sell them for a profit.
3. **Growth Equity**: Investing in more mature companies that need capital to expand, without the full-scale buyout structure.

Benefits of Private Equity:

- **High Return Potential**: Private equity investments, especially in successful startups or turnaround companies, can provide much higher returns than traditional investments.
- **Active Management**: Private equity firms often take a hands-on role in managing the companies they invest in, leading to operational improvements and increased value.

Risks of Private Equity:

- **Illiquidity**: Private equity investments are typically locked in for several years, making it difficult to exit the investment early.
- **High Fees**: Private equity firms often charge significant management and performance fees, which can erode returns.
- **Concentration Risk**: Private equity funds often make large, concentrated bets on individual companies, leading to greater risk if one investment fails.

Commodities

Commodities include physical assets such as **gold**, **oil**, **agricultural products**, and **metals**. Investing in commodities can be done directly (buying the physical asset) or indirectly through **commodity futures**, **exchange-traded funds (ETFs)**, or **mutual funds**. Commodities can act as a hedge against inflation and provide diversification, as their performance often differs from that of stocks and bonds.

Key Features of Commodities:

1. **Tangible Assets**: Commodities represent physical goods, providing intrinsic value.
2. **Global Demand**: Commodity prices are influenced by global supply and demand dynamics, geopolitical events, and economic trends.
3. **Volatility**: Commodity prices can be highly volatile due to factors such as weather conditions, geopolitical tensions, and changes in consumer demand.

Benefits of Commodities:

- **Inflation Hedge**: Commodities, particularly precious metals like gold, can protect against inflation as their prices often rise when inflation increases.
- **Portfolio Diversification**: Commodities tend to have low correlation with stocks and bonds, making them a valuable addition to a diversified portfolio.

Risks of Commodities:

- **High Volatility**: Commodity prices can fluctuate dramatically, often in response to unpredictable factors such as natural disasters or political events.
- **Storage and Transportation Costs**: For investors holding physical commodities, there are additional costs associated with storing and transporting the assets.
- **No Yield or Dividends**: Unlike stocks or bonds, commodities do not generate income in the form of dividends or interest.

Risks of Alternative Investments

Alternative assets offer diversification and the potential for higher returns, but they also come with unique risks that investors should carefully consider:

1. **Illiquidity**: Many alternative investments, especially hedge funds and private equity, have long lock-up periods, limiting access to your capital.
2. **High Fees**: Hedge funds and private equity firms often charge substantial fees that can significantly reduce net returns.
3. **Complexity**: Alternative strategies can be difficult to understand, and they may involve the use of derivatives, leverage, or other sophisticated tools.
4. **Regulatory Risks**: Alternative investments are often less regulated than traditional assets, which can lead to a lack of transparency and increased risk of fraud or mismanagement.

Conclusion: Are Alternative Investments Right for You?

Alternative investment strategies offer the potential for higher returns and diversification, but they are not suitable for all investors. They tend to be more complex, illiquid, and risky than traditional investments like stocks and bonds. If you are considering adding alternative assets to your portfolio, it's essential to:

- **Understand the Risks**: Make sure you fully comprehend the risks associated with each type of alternative investment.
- **Assess Your Time Horizon**: Many alternative investments require a long-term commitment, so ensure that you won't need to access the funds in the short term.
- **Evaluate Your Risk Tolerance**: Alternative assets can be highly volatile, so make sure you have the stomach for potential short-term losses in pursuit of long-term gains.

Ultimately, alternative investments should only be a small part of a well-diversified portfolio, complementing your more stable holdings in traditional stocks and bonds.

PART 4: BUILDING A PORTFOLIO

Risks of Alternative Investments

CHAPTER 13: ASSET ALLOCATION AND DIVERSIFICATION

A well-constructed investment portfolio is more than just a collection of individual stocks, bonds, or funds. It is an intentional blend of assets designed to balance risk and reward according to an investor's goals, risk tolerance, and time horizon. **Asset allocation** and **diversification** are the foundational principles of portfolio construction that allow investors to manage risk and optimize returns over time.

What is Asset Allocation?

Asset allocation refers to how an investor distributes their investments across different asset classes, such as **stocks**, **bonds**, **real estate**, and **cash equivalents**. The idea is to balance risk and reward by allocating different percentages of the portfolio to each asset class, depending on the investor's objectives and risk tolerance.

Key Asset Classes:

1. **Stocks (Equities)**: Provide the potential for high returns through capital appreciation, but come with higher volatility and risk. Best suited for investors with a longer time horizon.
2. **Bonds (Fixed Income)**: Offer more stability and income through interest payments, but with lower return potential than stocks. They are generally less volatile

and are often used to reduce portfolio risk.
3. **Real Estate**: Adds diversification through physical assets, offering income through rent and potential capital appreciation.
4. **Cash and Cash Equivalents**: Highly liquid, low-risk investments like savings accounts or money market funds, but they typically offer low returns. These are best for preserving capital and providing liquidity.

Why is Asset Allocation Important?

Asset allocation is crucial because different asset classes perform differently under various economic conditions. Stocks may outperform in a growing economy, while bonds can provide stability during economic downturns. By diversifying across asset classes, investors reduce the risk of significant losses in any one area of the portfolio.

Historical data shows that asset allocation decisions, rather than individual stock picking, are the most important determinant of a portfolio's long-term return.

Diversification: Spreading the Risk

While asset allocation determines how much to invest in each category, **diversification** involves spreading investments **within** those categories. The idea is to reduce risk by investing in a variety of securities so that the underperformance of one security doesn't drastically impact the entire portfolio.

How to Achieve Diversification:

1. **Within Asset Classes**:
   - In stocks, diversification can be achieved by investing in different sectors (e.g., technology, healthcare, energy) or geographies (domestic and international markets).
   - For bonds, you can diversify by investing in different types of bonds, such as government bonds, corporate bonds, and municipal bonds, or by choosing bonds

with different maturities.
2. **Across Asset Classes**:
  o   By mixing different asset classes like stocks, bonds, real estate, and commodities, you reduce the impact of market volatility. For instance, bonds may stabilize the portfolio when stocks are volatile.

Balancing Risk and Reward

Risk and reward are inextricably linked in investing. **Higher-risk assets** (like stocks) generally offer higher potential returns, but also come with more volatility. **Lower-risk assets** (like bonds or cash) offer more stability but have lower return potential. Finding the right balance is the goal of asset allocation.

Understanding Risk Tolerance:

Investors need to assess their **risk tolerance**—the level of volatility they are comfortable with—and their **time horizon**—how long they plan to hold their investments before needing access to the money. Younger investors, with a longer time horizon, can often afford to take on more risk because they have time to recover from market downturns. Older investors, especially those nearing retirement, may prioritize preserving their wealth, leading to more conservative allocations.

Risk Tolerance Types:

- **Conservative**: Prioritizes capital preservation, with a large allocation to bonds and cash, and a smaller portion in equities.
- **Moderate**: A balanced approach that typically includes a mix of stocks and bonds.
- **Aggressive**: A focus on capital growth, with a higher allocation to stocks and other high-risk assets, and a smaller allocation to bonds or cash.

Models for Portfolio Allocation

There are several popular models of asset allocation, ranging from conservative to aggressive. These models help investors decide how to allocate their portfolio based on their risk tolerance and investment goals.

Conservative Portfolio:

- **20% Stocks, 80% Bonds/Cash**: Designed for risk-averse investors or those nearing retirement, this portfolio prioritizes stability and income over growth. It will likely generate lower returns but will also experience less volatility.

Balanced Portfolio:

- **60% Stocks, 40% Bonds**: A balanced portfolio is suited for moderate investors who want a mix of growth and income. This portfolio provides a reasonable opportunity for capital appreciation while managing risk.

Aggressive Portfolio:

- **80% Stocks, 20% Bonds/Cash**: This allocation is for investors with a high tolerance for risk and a long time horizon. It emphasizes growth through equities, with bonds serving as a cushion during downturns.

Lifecycle/Target-Date Funds:

These funds automatically adjust asset allocation over time based on the investor's age or target retirement date. Early on, the fund may be aggressive, with a higher allocation to stocks. As the investor approaches retirement, the fund gradually shifts to a more conservative allocation, focusing more on bonds and cash equivalents.

Rebalancing: Keeping Your Portfolio on Track

Over time, the performance of your investments will likely cause your portfolio to drift from its original allocation. For example, if stocks perform well, they may make up a larger percentage of your portfolio than intended, increasing your overall risk exposure. To maintain your desired risk profile, it's essential to **rebalance** your portfolio periodically.

How to Rebalance:

1. **Review Your Portfolio**: Check your portfolio allocation regularly (e.g., once a year) to see if it has drifted significantly from your target allocation.
2. **Sell or Buy Assets**: If one asset class has grown too large, you can sell some of those investments and reinvest the proceeds in underweighted asset classes to restore balance.
3. **Use New Contributions**: Instead of selling assets, you can rebalance by directing new contributions to the underweighted parts of your portfolio.

Conclusion: The Importance of Asset Allocation and Diversification

The combination of smart asset allocation and diversification is one of the most effective strategies for managing risk while aiming for long-term growth. Whether you are building a portfolio from scratch or refining your existing investments, understanding these principles is key to achieving your financial goals. By finding the right balance of asset classes, diversifying within those classes, and periodically rebalancing your portfolio, you can protect your investments from market volatility while maximizing your potential for return.

In the next chapters, we will dive deeper into specific strategies for creating portfolios tailored to various financial objectives, such as retirement, education savings, and wealth preservation.

CHAPTER 14: RISK MANAGEMENT AND HEDGING

Investing always involves risk, but effective risk management strategies can help reduce potential losses, particularly during market downturns. One of the most critical aspects of risk management is knowing how to **hedge**—using specific techniques and financial instruments to protect your portfolio from adverse market movements. In this chapter, we'll explore the key concepts of risk management, including hedging through **options** and using **safe-haven assets** to provide stability.

Why Risk Management Matters

Every investment comes with some degree of risk, whether from **market volatility**, **interest rate changes**, **economic cycles**, or **geopolitical events**. While it's impossible to eliminate risk entirely, investors can take steps to minimize its impact on their portfolios. Effective risk management can help:

- **Protect Capital**: By reducing the potential for large losses, investors can protect their wealth during periods of market turbulence.
- **Reduce Volatility**: Hedging strategies can help smooth out the fluctuations in portfolio value, providing more consistent returns.
- **Enhance Long-Term Returns**: Avoiding large losses allows your portfolio to recover faster and compounds returns over

time.

Protecting Against Market Downturns

One of the key elements of risk management is preparing for the possibility of a market downturn. While markets tend to rise over the long term, they can be volatile in the short term, and significant losses can derail financial goals.

Diversification:

As discussed in earlier chapters, diversification is one of the simplest ways to manage risk. By spreading investments across different asset classes (such as stocks, bonds, and real estate), sectors, and geographic regions, investors reduce their exposure to any single market event.

Portfolio Rebalancing:

Regularly rebalancing your portfolio ensures that you maintain the desired allocation of assets, even as markets fluctuate. Rebalancing can prevent overexposure to riskier assets, particularly after a period of strong market performance.

Hedging with Options

Options are financial instruments that give investors the right, but not the obligation, to buy or sell an asset at a predetermined price within a specific period. They can be a valuable tool for **hedging**, allowing investors to protect against potential losses in their portfolios.

Key Types of Options:

1. **Call Options**: Give the holder the right to buy an asset (e.g., a stock) at a predetermined price (the strike price) before the option expires. Investors typically use call options when they expect the price of the asset to rise.
2. **Put Options**: Give the holder the right to sell an asset at a predetermined price before the option expires. Put options are often used to hedge against a decline in the value of a stock or portfolio.

How to Use Options for Hedging:

- **Protecting Individual Stocks**: If you own a stock and are concerned about a short-term decline, you can purchase a **put option** on that stock. If the stock's price falls, the value of the put option will rise, offsetting some or all of your losses.
- **Portfolio Insurance**: Investors can use **index put options** to protect against a broad market decline. For example, if you hold a diversified portfolio of stocks, buying a put option on a major index like the S&P 500 can serve as insurance against market-wide losses.

Costs and Considerations:

- **Premiums**: Options come with a cost, known as the **premium**, which is the price paid to purchase the option. Investors need to weigh this cost against the potential benefit of the protection it provides.
- **Expiration**: Options have expiration dates, meaning they only provide protection for a limited time. If the market doesn't move as expected within that period, the option may expire worthless.

While options can be an effective hedging tool, they can also be complex and risky if not used correctly. It's important to have a solid understanding of how they work before incorporating them into a risk management strategy.

Using Safe-Haven Assets

In addition to options, many investors turn to **safe-haven assets** to protect their portfolios during periods of market uncertainty. Safe-haven assets are those that tend to maintain or increase in value during market downturns, providing stability when other investments are volatile.

Common Safe-Haven Assets:

1. **Gold**: Often seen as a store of value, gold has historically performed well during periods of economic instability

or inflation. Investors can gain exposure to gold through physical ownership, exchange-traded funds (ETFs), or gold mining stocks.
2. **Treasury Bonds**: U.S. **Treasury bonds**, particularly long-term Treasuries, are considered one of the safest investments because they are backed by the U.S. government. When markets are volatile, investors often flock to Treasuries for their stability and steady income.
3. **Cash and Cash Equivalents**: Holding cash, or investing in cash equivalents such as money market funds, can provide liquidity and protection from market downturns. While cash doesn't offer growth, it preserves capital and allows for quick redeployment into investments when opportunities arise.

Benefits of Safe-Haven Assets:

- **Stability**: Safe-haven assets tend to be less volatile than stocks, providing a cushion during periods of market stress.
- **Liquidity**: Many safe-haven assets, such as cash and Treasury bonds, are highly liquid, making it easy to access your funds when needed.
- **Diversification**: Adding safe-haven assets to a portfolio can help reduce overall risk and smooth returns over time.

Limitations of Safe-Haven Assets:

- **Lower Returns**: Safe-haven assets typically offer lower returns than riskier investments like stocks. Holding too much of your portfolio in these assets can limit long-term growth potential.
- **Inflation Risk**: Assets like cash and bonds may not keep pace with inflation, eroding purchasing power over time.

Tailoring Risk Management to Your Portfolio

The appropriate risk management strategy depends on an individual's investment goals, risk tolerance, and time horizon. For some, simple diversification and periodic rebalancing may provide sufficient protection. For others, more advanced strategies like options or safe-haven assets may be necessary.

Risk Tolerance Assessment:

Understanding your risk tolerance is critical when deciding how to manage risk. Investors with a low tolerance for volatility might want to allocate a larger portion of their portfolio to bonds, cash, or safe-haven assets. Conversely, those with a higher risk tolerance may be comfortable holding more equities and using hedging techniques like options to mitigate risk.

Time Horizon Considerations:

The time horizon for your investments also plays a key role in risk management. Investors with long-term goals, such as retirement, can typically afford to take on more risk and ride out short-term market fluctuations. On the other hand, those with shorter time horizons, like individuals nearing retirement, may prioritize capital preservation and need to implement more robust hedging strategies.

Conclusion: Integrating Risk Management into Your Investment Strategy

No investment strategy is complete without considering how to manage risk. Whether through diversification, the use of options, or the incorporation of safe-haven assets, effective risk management can protect your portfolio from significant losses and help you achieve your financial goals. By understanding the various tools and techniques available, you can tailor a risk management approach that fits your specific needs and preferences.

In the next chapter, we will discuss how to evaluate the performance of your investments and how to adjust your portfolio over time to stay on track with your goals.

CHAPTER 15: THE PSYCHOLOGY OF INVESTING

Investing is not only about numbers, charts, and financial strategies—it also involves a deep understanding of human psychology. Often, our emotions and behavioral biases influence investment decisions in ways that may not align with rational, long-term financial goals. This chapter explores the psychology of investing, focusing on common behavioral biases and emotional pitfalls, and offers strategies for maintaining discipline in the face of market volatility and uncertainty.

Behavioral Biases in Investing

Behavioral biases are cognitive distortions that affect how we perceive information and make decisions. In investing, these biases can lead to poor decisions that ultimately hurt returns. Recognizing and overcoming these biases is critical for successful long-term investing.

1. Loss Aversion:

Loss aversion is the tendency to fear losses more than we value equivalent gains. Studies show that the psychological pain of losing money is roughly twice as powerful as the pleasure of making money. As a result, investors often avoid selling losing investments, hoping they will rebound, or panic-sell during a downturn, locking in losses rather than waiting for a recovery.

- Example: An investor might hold on to a stock that has

dropped 20% in value, hoping it will recover, even though selling and reallocating to a better-performing investment could be a wiser decision.
- Strategy: To combat loss aversion, it's important to set clear rules for when to sell a stock, such as based on a specific percentage drop or a change in the company's fundamentals. Having a pre-determined exit strategy can prevent emotional decision-making.

2. Overconfidence:

Many investors overestimate their ability to predict market movements or pick winning stocks. This overconfidence bias can lead to excessive trading, higher transaction costs, and poor long-term performance.

- Example: An investor might believe they can consistently "beat the market" by picking individual stocks, even though research shows that most professional investors struggle to do so over time.
- Strategy: Recognize the limits of your knowledge and expertise. Diversifying across a broad range of assets, or opting for passive strategies like index funds, can mitigate the impact of overconfidence.

3. Herd Mentality:

Herd mentality occurs when investors follow the actions of the majority, often driven by fear or excitement, rather than by rational analysis. This can lead to bubbles (when asset prices become overinflated) or crashes (when panic selling drives prices down).

- Example: During the dot-com bubble, many investors piled into tech stocks because "everyone else" was doing it, even though many companies had questionable financials. This eventually led to a market crash.
- Strategy: It's crucial to focus on the fundamentals of your investments rather than following market trends or the

latest "hot stock." Independent analysis and sticking to your investment plan can help you avoid costly mistakes.

4. Anchoring:

Anchoring refers to the human tendency to rely too heavily on the first piece of information encountered when making decisions. In investing, this often manifests as an investor anchoring on a stock's past price, making it difficult to objectively assess its current value.

- Example: An investor might refuse to sell a stock that is currently trading at $50, believing it should eventually return to its previous high of $100, despite changes in the company's prospects.
- Strategy: Focus on the future potential of an investment rather than its past performance. Reassess your holdings regularly based on current data and market conditions.

Emotional Pitfalls in Investing

While behavioral biases skew our decisions, emotions often drive impulsive reactions that conflict with long-term investment success. Fear, greed, and impatience are among the most common emotional pitfalls.

1. Fear:

Fear can cause investors to sell during market downturns, turning paper losses into real ones. During periods of volatility, emotions can overwhelm rational decision-making, leading to panic selling that locks in losses.

- Example: In the 2008 financial crisis, many investors sold their holdings at the bottom of the market, missing out on the subsequent recovery.
- Strategy: Having a long-term plan and sticking to it can help manage fear. If you're investing for retirement 20 years from now, a temporary market dip is unlikely to affect your ultimate outcome. It's also helpful to set up automatic contributions to your investment accounts, so you stay

invested regardless of market conditions.

2. Greed:

Greed can lead investors to take on excessive risk, especially when markets are rising, in the hope of generating higher returns. This often results in chasing speculative investments or high-flying stocks at inflated prices.

- Example: During bull markets, investors may be tempted to put money into overvalued assets like cryptocurrencies or speculative tech stocks, ignoring the risks.
- Strategy: Diversification is a key defense against greed. Rather than chasing the latest investment fad, spread your portfolio across asset classes to ensure you are not overexposed to any single high-risk investment. Additionally, maintaining realistic return expectations can prevent you from making impulsive, high-risk decisions.

3. Impatience:

Investing requires patience, as building wealth takes time. However, many investors become impatient when they don't see immediate results, leading them to switch strategies or sell prematurely.

- Example: An investor might sell a mutual fund after a year of mediocre returns, despite having a long-term investment horizon, missing out on future gains.
- Strategy: Focus on your long-term goals and ignore short-term market noise. Set clear time horizons for your investments, and review them periodically rather than reacting to every fluctuation in the market.

Strategies to Maintain Discipline

The best way to combat behavioral biases and emotional pitfalls is to establish clear strategies that promote discipline and long-term thinking. Here are a few practical steps you can take to maintain discipline in your investing journey:

1. Create a Solid Investment Plan:

Develop an investment plan based on your goals, time horizon, and risk tolerance. A well-structured plan will help you avoid making decisions based on short-term market movements. Include guidelines for asset allocation, rebalancing, and when to buy or sell.

2. Automate Your Investments:

Setting up automatic contributions to your investment accounts (such as through a 401(k) or other retirement plan) ensures that you consistently invest, regardless of market conditions. This approach also takes advantage of dollar-cost averaging, which helps reduce the impact of market volatility over time.

3. Monitor Your Emotions:

Be aware of your emotional state when making investment decisions. If you feel anxious or overly excited about the market, take a step back and review your long-term plan. Avoid making hasty decisions in response to fear or greed.

4. Stick to a Long-Term Perspective:

Investing is a marathon, not a sprint. Markets will experience ups and downs, but over time, they tend to rise. Keeping a long-term perspective helps you ride out short-term volatility and stay focused on your ultimate goals.

5. Rebalance Regularly:

Rebalancing your portfolio periodically ensures that you maintain your desired risk profile. If certain asset classes outperform others, they may become a larger portion of your portfolio, increasing your risk. Rebalancing helps you stick to your original allocation and prevents emotional decisions.

6. Educate Yourself:

The more you know about investing, the better equipped you are to avoid common mistakes. Regularly reading about market trends, behavioral finance, and investment strategies can help you make more informed decisions and stay disciplined during uncertain times.

Conclusion: The Power of Discipline in Investing

Successful investing requires more than just financial knowledge—it demands discipline and the ability to control emotional impulses. By recognizing common behavioral biases and emotional pitfalls, and implementing strategies to manage them, you can stay focused on your long-term goals and make smarter decisions. Whether through a solid investment plan, automation, or regular rebalancing, maintaining discipline will help you navigate the ups and downs of the market and increase your chances of achieving financial success.

In the final part of the book, we will explore how to measure investment performance and adjust your strategy over time to stay on track toward your goals.

PART 5: LONG-TERM INVESTMENT PLANNING

CHAPTER 16: SETTING FINANCIAL GOALS

Investing successfully starts with setting clear, actionable financial goals. Without a destination in mind, it's easy to get distracted by short-term market movements and lose sight of what matters most—achieving your personal and financial objectives. In this chapter, we will discuss how to define and achieve **short**, **medium**, and **long-term goals**, as well as highlight the critical role that **budgeting** and **saving** play in the process.

Defining Financial Goals

Financial goals can be categorized based on the time it takes to achieve them. Each category—short, medium, and long-term—requires different investment strategies and approaches.

1. Short-Term Goals (1–3 Years)

Short-term goals are those you plan to achieve within the next few years. These might include:

- Saving for a vacation
- Building an emergency fund
- Buying a new car

Because these goals have a shorter time horizon, the focus should be on **capital preservation** rather than maximizing returns. Investing in low-risk, **liquid** assets such as money market funds, savings accounts, or short-term government bonds is often the best approach.

2. Medium-Term Goals (3–7 Years)

Medium-term goals fall in the range of 3 to 7 years and may include:

- Saving for a down payment on a home
- Funding a child's education
- Paying off debt

For medium-term goals, you can take on a bit more risk than with short-term goals, but you should still prioritize **moderate risk** and **stability**. A balanced portfolio of **stocks and bonds** or **conservative mutual funds** is often appropriate. The aim is to grow your capital while minimizing the potential for significant losses.

3. Long-Term Goals (7+ Years)

Long-term goals are those that will take more than seven years to achieve. Examples include:

- Saving for retirement
- Paying for your child's university education
- Building generational wealth

For long-term goals, you can afford to take on more risk since you have a longer time horizon to recover from market downturns. **Growth-oriented investments**, such as **stocks**, **equity mutual funds**, and **real estate**, are ideal for long-term goals. Over time, these assets have the potential to offer higher returns, benefiting from **compounding** and market growth.

How to Achieve Your Financial Goals

Achieving financial goals requires a structured plan that includes both **saving** and **investing**. The key steps to turn your goals into reality include:

1. Prioritize Your Goals

Begin by listing your financial goals and **prioritizing** them based on importance and time horizon. Ask yourself:

- Which goals are essential, such as retirement or an

emergency fund?
- Which goals are desirable but not critical, such as a luxury vacation?
- When do I need to achieve each goal?

By prioritizing, you can allocate resources effectively and ensure that you're focusing on what matters most.

2. Create a Budget

A budget is the foundation of any financial plan. It helps you track your income, control your spending, and allocate money toward your goals. Without a clear budget, it's easy to spend more than you earn, leaving little room for saving or investing.

Steps to create a budget:

- **Track your income and expenses**: Record all sources of income and categorize your spending into essential (rent, groceries, utilities) and non-essential (dining out, entertainment).
- **Set spending limits**: Identify areas where you can cut back, and allocate those savings toward your financial goals.
- **Pay yourself first**: Make saving and investing a priority by setting aside a portion of your income (e.g., 10-20%) before spending on non-essential items.

3. Establish a Savings Plan

Saving is a critical first step toward achieving your financial goals. Even before you begin investing, it's essential to build an **emergency fund** and have enough cash reserves to cover unforeseen expenses.

Steps to build a savings plan:

- **Set a savings target**: Aim to save at least three to six months' worth of living expenses in an emergency fund.
- **Automate your savings**: Set up automatic transfers from your checking account to a dedicated savings account to ensure consistent contributions.

- **Earn interest on your savings**: Park your emergency fund in a high-interest savings account or a money market fund to earn a modest return while keeping your money accessible.

4. Invest for Growth

Once your emergency fund is in place and you have a savings plan, you can begin investing. Investing allows your money to grow over time and is essential for reaching long-term goals like retirement.

Key considerations when investing:

- **Risk tolerance**: Understand your comfort level with market fluctuations and choose investments accordingly. Stocks offer higher returns but are more volatile, while bonds are more stable but provide lower returns.
- **Diversification**: Spread your investments across different asset classes (stocks, bonds, real estate) and sectors to reduce risk.
- **Review regularly**: Periodically assess your portfolio to ensure it aligns with your goals and time horizon. Rebalance if necessary to maintain your target allocation.

The Importance of Budgeting and Saving

Achieving financial goals isn't just about investing wisely; it's about living within your means and making sure you're saving enough to fund your future. **Budgeting** and **saving** are the cornerstones of any financial plan and play a crucial role in the following areas:

1. Budgeting Helps Control Spending

A budget forces you to be mindful of your spending habits. By creating a clear plan for where your money goes each month, you can identify areas where you might be overspending and redirect those funds toward more important goals. Budgeting also ensures you don't rely on credit cards or loans to fund your lifestyle, reducing debt and interest payments.

2. Saving Builds Financial Security

Saving provides a safety net that protects you from unexpected events, such as job loss, medical emergencies, or home repairs. Without sufficient savings, you may be forced to dip into your investment accounts or take on debt, derailing your financial progress.

3. Saving Enables Investment Opportunities

Investing is the key to long-term wealth creation, but you can't invest if you don't have the funds. By consistently saving a portion of your income, you create the capital needed to invest in growth-oriented assets. The earlier you start saving and investing, the more you can benefit from **compound interest**—earning interest on both your initial savings and the interest that accumulates over time.

Setting SMART Financial Goals

To make your financial goals more actionable, consider using the **SMART** framework. SMART goals are:

- **Specific**: Clearly define what you want to achieve (e.g., "Save $50,000 for a house down payment").
- **Measurable**: Establish criteria for measuring progress (e.g., "Contribute $500 per month to my savings account").
- **Achievable**: Set realistic goals that are within your capacity (e.g., "Save 15% of my income after reducing discretionary spending").
- **Relevant**: Ensure your goals align with your overall financial objectives (e.g., "Saving for a house will help me build equity and stop renting").
- **Time-bound**: Set a deadline for achieving your goals (e.g., "Reach $50,000 in savings within four years").

Using the SMART framework ensures that your financial goals are well-defined, actionable, and attainable.

Conclusion: Building a Path to Financial Success

Setting clear, actionable financial goals is the foundation of successful investing. By defining short, medium, and long-term goals, creating a budget, and establishing a disciplined saving and investing strategy, you can take control of your financial future. Remember, financial goals are not set in stone—your priorities and circumstances may change over time. Regularly review your goals, adjust your strategy as needed, and stay committed to your long-term plan.

In the next chapter, we'll explore how to monitor and measure your investment performance, ensuring that you stay on track to achieve your financial objectives.

PART 4: RISK MANAGEMENT AND PSYCHOLOGY

CHAPTER 17: RETIREMENT PLANNING

Planning for retirement is one of the most important financial goals you'll face. A well-designed retirement plan ensures that you can maintain your lifestyle and financial independence when you stop working. This chapter will focus on building and managing a **retirement portfolio**, as well as understanding the role of **tax-advantaged retirement accounts**.

Building a Retirement Portfolio

A retirement portfolio is simply the collection of investments that you use to fund your retirement. The key to building a successful retirement portfolio is balancing **growth** and **stability**, while accounting for your **risk tolerance**, **time horizon**, and **income needs** in retirement.

1. Determine Your Time Horizon

Your **time horizon**—the number of years until you plan to retire—plays a crucial role in determining how aggressively or conservatively you should invest.

- **Long-term horizon (20+ years)**: If you have several decades until retirement, you can afford to take on more risk, as you have time to recover from market downturns. A higher allocation to **stocks** is typically recommended, as they offer the potential for long-term growth.
- **Medium-term horizon (10-20 years)**: As retirement

approaches, you may want to reduce your exposure to riskier assets like stocks and gradually shift toward more **bonds** and **fixed income** to preserve capital.
- **Short-term horizon (less than 10 years)**: With retirement around the corner, capital preservation becomes the priority. You'll want to reduce volatility by focusing on lower-risk investments such as **bonds**, **cash**, or **stable value funds** to avoid significant losses right before you begin withdrawals.

2. Asset Allocation

Asset allocation refers to how you divide your investments among different asset classes, such as stocks, bonds, and cash. For retirement planning, this allocation should evolve as your time horizon shortens and your tolerance for risk decreases.

- **Stocks for growth**: Stocks are the primary engine for growing your retirement portfolio. They tend to deliver higher long-term returns compared to bonds and cash, but they also come with more volatility.
- **Bonds for stability**: Bonds offer more predictable returns and help reduce the overall volatility of your portfolio. As you near retirement, increasing your bond allocation provides stability and income.
- **Cash for liquidity**: Keeping some portion of your retirement savings in cash or cash equivalents (such as money market funds) ensures you have liquidity for immediate expenses, especially during the early years of retirement.

3. Diversification

Diversification is key to reducing risk in your retirement portfolio. By spreading your investments across different asset classes, sectors, and geographies, you can avoid overexposure to any one area of the market. A well-diversified portfolio typically includes:

- **U.S. stocks** and **international stocks** for growth potential
- **Government and corporate bonds** for income and stability

- **Real estate** (through direct ownership or REITs) for diversification and inflation protection
- **Alternative assets** (like commodities or hedge funds) for further risk mitigation, depending on your risk tolerance

4. Rebalancing Your Portfolio

As you move closer to retirement, you should regularly **rebalance** your portfolio to maintain your target asset allocation. Rebalancing involves selling assets that have outperformed and buying those that have underperformed, keeping your portfolio in line with your risk tolerance and financial goals.

For example, if stocks perform well and grow to represent 80% of your portfolio (when your target was 60%), you might sell some stocks and buy bonds to bring the portfolio back to your intended allocation.

Managing Your Retirement Portfolio in Retirement

Once you retire, managing your portfolio shifts from accumulating wealth to generating a steady income. The goal is to ensure your savings last throughout your retirement years.

1. Withdrawal Strategy

The **4% rule** is a common guideline for withdrawing from your retirement savings. It suggests withdrawing 4% of your portfolio's value in the first year of retirement, adjusting for inflation in subsequent years. This approach aims to provide a steady income stream while minimizing the risk of running out of money over a 30-year retirement.

- **Example**: If you have a $1 million retirement portfolio, the 4% rule suggests withdrawing $40,000 in your first year of retirement. Each following year, you would adjust this amount for inflation.

2. Generating Retirement Income

Your retirement portfolio can generate income in various ways:

- **Dividends** from stocks

- **Interest** from bonds
- **Real estate income** from rental properties or REITs
- **Systematic withdrawals** from your investment accounts

It's important to create a balance between drawing income from your portfolio while preserving enough principal to sustain you throughout retirement.

3. Managing Risk in Retirement

In retirement, **sequence-of-returns risk** becomes more important. This refers to the risk that poor market returns early in retirement could significantly reduce the value of your portfolio. To mitigate this risk, consider:

- Holding **2–3 years of living expenses** in cash or short-term bonds to avoid selling assets at a loss during market downturns
- Gradually reducing your exposure to stocks as you progress through retirement

Tax-Advantaged Retirement Accounts

Tax-advantaged accounts are a cornerstone of retirement planning, as they offer significant tax benefits that can help your savings grow faster. There are two main types: **traditional accounts** (where contributions are tax-deferred) and **Roth accounts** (where contributions are made with after-tax dollars).

1. Traditional Accounts

- **401(k) or 403(b)**: Employer-sponsored retirement accounts allow you to contribute pre-tax dollars, reducing your taxable income for the year. Your investments grow tax-deferred, and you pay taxes only when you withdraw funds in retirement. Employers often offer a **matching contribution**, which is essentially free money.
- **Traditional IRA**: An individual retirement account that works similarly to a 401(k) but is not employer-sponsored. Contributions may be tax-deductible, depending on your income level, and you won't pay taxes until you withdraw

funds.
- **Withdrawals**: Distributions from traditional accounts are taxed as ordinary income. Required minimum distributions (RMDs) must begin at age 73, meaning you must start withdrawing a certain amount each year.

2. Roth Accounts

- **Roth 401(k)** or **Roth IRA**: Contributions to Roth accounts are made with after-tax dollars, meaning you don't get an immediate tax deduction, but the benefit is that your investments grow **tax-free**, and withdrawals in retirement are also tax-free, provided certain conditions are met.
- **No RMDs for Roth IRAs**: Unlike traditional accounts, Roth IRAs do not have required minimum distributions, giving you more flexibility in managing your withdrawals.
- **Best for younger investors**: Roth accounts are particularly beneficial for younger investors who expect to be in a higher tax bracket in retirement. Paying taxes now can result in significant savings later.

3. Contribution Limits

Retirement accounts have annual contribution limits, which can change from year to year. In 2024, the limits are:

- **401(k)**: $23,000 for individuals under age 50, with an additional $7,500 in catch-up contributions allowed for those 50 and older.
- **IRA**: $7,000 for individuals under 50, with an additional $1,000 catch-up contribution for those over 50.

Conclusion: Planning for a Secure Retirement

Building and managing a retirement portfolio requires careful planning, consistent saving, and smart investment decisions. By understanding your time horizon, maintaining a diversified portfolio, and taking advantage of tax-advantaged accounts, you can maximize your retirement savings and ensure financial security in your later years.

In the final chapters, we will explore how to monitor your portfolio performance and adjust your investment strategy over time to stay on track toward a comfortable retirement.

CHAPTER 18: TAX-EFFICIENT INVESTING

Investing can generate significant returns, but taxes can take a large bite out of those gains if you're not careful. **Tax-efficient investing** is the practice of structuring your investments to minimize the impact of taxes, allowing you to keep more of your returns. In this chapter, we'll explore strategies such as reducing taxes on **gains and dividends**, as well as techniques like **tax-loss harvesting** and utilizing **tax-deferred accounts**.

1. Reducing Taxes on Gains and Dividends

There are two main types of taxes investors encounter: **capital gains taxes** and **dividend taxes**.

Capital Gains Taxes

Capital gains taxes apply to the profit you make when you sell an asset. The rate you pay depends on how long you've held the asset:

- **Short-term capital gains**: These apply when you sell an asset you've held for less than a year. The gains are taxed at your **ordinary income tax rate**, which could be as high as 37% for high earners.
- **Long-term capital gains**: If you hold an asset for more than a year before selling, you'll be taxed at the more favorable **long-term capital gains rates**, which range from 0% to 20%, depending on your income.

Strategy: By holding investments for longer than a year, you can benefit from the lower long-term capital gains rates and significantly reduce the taxes on your profits.

Dividend Taxes

Dividends are another source of taxable income. Dividends are categorized as either **qualified** or **ordinary**:

- **Qualified dividends**: These are taxed at the lower long-term capital gains rates.
- **Ordinary dividends**: These are taxed as regular income, which can be a higher rate depending on your tax bracket.

Strategy: Investing in companies that pay **qualified dividends** or holding dividend-paying investments in **tax-advantaged accounts** (like IRAs or 401(k)s) can help reduce your overall tax burden.

2. Tax-Loss Harvesting

Tax-loss harvesting is a technique used to offset taxable gains by selling investments that have lost value. Here's how it works:

- If you have sold investments for a profit, you can sell other investments that are currently worth less than what you paid for them. The loss from the sale can be used to offset your taxable gains, reducing the amount of taxes you owe.
- If your losses exceed your gains, you can deduct up to $3,000 of those losses against your ordinary income, and any remaining losses can be carried forward to future tax years.

Strategy: Regularly review your portfolio for underperforming assets that you can sell to generate tax losses, especially toward the end of the tax year.

3. Tax-Deferred Investments

Tax-deferred accounts like **401(k)s**, **IRAs**, and **annuities** allow your investments to grow without incurring taxes until you withdraw the funds in retirement. This can be a powerful way to compound your returns more quickly, as taxes on dividends, interest, and capital gains are postponed.

Strategy: Maximize contributions to tax-deferred accounts each year to take full advantage of these tax benefits. When withdrawing funds in retirement, you may be in a lower tax bracket, which could further reduce the taxes you pay.

4. Municipal Bonds for Tax-Free Income

Municipal bonds, issued by local and state governments, offer a key tax advantage: their interest income is typically exempt from federal taxes and, in some cases, state and local taxes as well. While municipal bonds generally offer lower yields than taxable bonds, the tax benefits can make them an attractive option for high-income investors.

Strategy: For those in higher tax brackets, consider adding municipal bonds to your portfolio as a way to generate tax-free income.

Conclusion: Keep More of Your Returns

Minimizing the taxes you pay on investments is an essential part of any investment strategy. By holding investments for the long term, taking advantage of tax-loss harvesting, and using tax-deferred accounts, you can significantly reduce the impact of taxes on your portfolio and keep more of your hard-earned gains.

CHAPTER 19: SOCIALLY RESPONSIBLE INVESTING (SRI)

As awareness of environmental, social, and governance (ESG) issues grows, many investors are looking to align their investments with their personal values. **Socially Responsible Investing (SRI)** or **ESG investing** seeks to generate financial returns while also promoting ethical, social, and environmental causes. This chapter will introduce ESG investing and discuss how to balance **ethics** with **returns**.

1. What is ESG Investing?

ESG investing involves selecting investments based on a company's performance in three key areas:

- **Environmental**: How does the company impact the environment? This includes issues like carbon emissions, waste management, and renewable energy usage.
- **Social**: How does the company treat its employees, customers, and the communities in which it operates? Factors such as labor practices, diversity, and community involvement are considered.
- **Governance**: How is the company governed? Good corporate governance includes transparency, accountability, and strong ethical practices in leadership and decision-

making.

Example: An ESG-conscious investor might choose to invest in companies that prioritize sustainability, ethical labor practices, and strong corporate governance, while avoiding companies with poor environmental records or questionable labor practices.

2. Types of Socially Responsible Investments

There are several ways to implement an ESG or socially responsible investing strategy:

1. ESG-Focused Mutual Funds and ETFs

Many mutual funds and **ETFs** are specifically designed to include companies with high ESG ratings. These funds allow investors to gain exposure to a diversified portfolio of companies that meet specific ethical and sustainability criteria.

Strategy: Look for funds that have been certified or verified by third-party ESG rating agencies, ensuring they adhere to strict ESG principles.

2. Impact Investing

Impact investing goes beyond simply avoiding harmful companies and focuses on actively investing in companies or projects that are working to solve environmental and social problems. For example, an impact investor might fund companies developing clean energy solutions or affordable housing.

Strategy: Impact investing is best suited for investors who want their investments to actively drive positive change, even if it means potentially accepting lower returns.

3. Negative Screening

In **negative screening**, investors actively avoid certain industries or companies that don't align with their values. This might include excluding companies involved in fossil fuels, tobacco, weapons manufacturing, or unethical labor practices.

Strategy: Many ESG funds use negative screening to avoid companies with poor ethical practices or environmental records.

3. Balancing Ethics with Returns

One of the key concerns for ESG investors is whether they can achieve competitive financial returns while investing ethically. In the past, some argued that prioritizing ESG factors could lead to lower returns, but recent studies have shown that ESG-focused investments can perform as well as, or even better than, traditional investments.

Why ESG Investing Can Be Profitable:

- **Long-term risk reduction**: Companies with strong ESG practices are often better managed, less likely to face regulatory penalties, and more resilient in the face of environmental or social risks.
- **Growing demand**: As more investors and consumers prioritize sustainability, companies with high ESG ratings are becoming increasingly attractive, potentially leading to higher returns.

Strategy: ESG investors should continue to prioritize **diversification** and **risk management** while ensuring that the companies or funds they invest in meet their ethical standards. Over time, this approach can help balance social responsibility with financial success.

Conclusion: Investing with Purpose

Socially responsible investing allows investors to align their portfolios with their personal values, without necessarily sacrificing returns. Whether through ESG-focused funds, impact investing, or negative screening, there are many ways to create a portfolio that promotes ethical practices while still achieving long-term financial growth.

CHAPTER 20: ANALYZING MARKET CYCLES

Financial markets don't move in a straight line. They go through cycles of growth (booms) and contraction (busts). Understanding **market cycles** is crucial for making informed investment decisions and avoiding emotional reactions that could harm your long-term portfolio performance. In this chapter, we will look at the **boom-bust cycle**, **long-term market trends**, and key lessons from **past market crises**.

1. The Boom-Bust Cycle

Markets tend to follow a predictable cycle of expansion (booms) and contraction (busts). Recognizing the stages of this cycle can help investors make better decisions and avoid being caught off guard by sharp downturns.

Boom Phase

In a boom phase, the economy grows steadily, corporate profits increase, and stock markets rise. Investor confidence is high, and risk appetite grows, leading to increased investment in equities, real estate, and other assets. Booms are often fueled by:

- **Low interest rates**: These make borrowing cheaper and stimulate consumer and business spending.
- **Strong economic indicators**: Growth in GDP, low unemployment, and rising corporate earnings signal a healthy economy.

Risks during booms: Overconfidence can lead to speculative bubbles, where asset prices become detached from their intrinsic value. When the boom ends, the correction can be swift and painful.

Bust Phase

During a bust, the economy slows down, corporate profits decline, and stock markets fall. Investor sentiment turns negative, and risk aversion increases. Busts can be triggered by:

- **Rising interest rates**: Higher rates increase borrowing costs and reduce consumer spending.
- **Negative economic indicators**: Rising unemployment, declining GDP, or a sharp drop in corporate earnings can signal the start of a downturn.

Strategy during busts: Defensive assets like **bonds**, **cash**, and **safe-haven investments** (such as gold) tend to perform better during market downturns.

2. Long-Term Market Trends

Despite short-term cycles of booms and busts, markets tend to rise over the long term. This is driven by factors like:

- **Technological innovation**: New technologies create efficiencies, lower costs, and generate new industries, boosting economic growth.
- **Population growth**: An expanding population increases demand for goods and services, driving corporate profits and market growth.
- **Productivity improvements**: As companies become more efficient, their profitability improves, which benefits shareholders.

Key Lesson: Time in the market beats timing the market. While market cycles can create volatility in the short term, long-term investors typically benefit from staying invested through the ups and downs, allowing them to capture growth over time.

3. Lessons from Past Market Crises

Looking at historical market crises provides valuable insights into how markets behave during extreme downturns and recoveries.

The Dot-Com Bubble (1999-2000)

The late 1990s saw a massive rise in internet and technology stocks, leading to a speculative bubble. Many companies with little or no earnings achieved sky-high valuations. When the bubble burst, the tech-heavy NASDAQ index lost nearly 80% of its value.

Lesson: Avoid chasing speculative bubbles. Valuations matter, and markets eventually correct when asset prices become detached from fundamentals.

The Global Financial Crisis (2008-2009)

This crisis was triggered by the collapse of the housing market and the resulting failure of large financial institutions. Stock markets worldwide plummeted, and global economies entered a severe recession.

Lesson: Diversification and risk management are essential. Markets can experience severe downturns, but those who stayed invested and focused on long-term goals saw a recovery.

COVID-19 Market Crash (2020)

The COVID-19 pandemic caused a rapid selloff in global markets in early 2020. However, the markets quickly rebounded as central banks and governments provided unprecedented stimulus, leading to one of the fastest recoveries in market history.

Lesson: Stay disciplined and avoid panic selling. Markets are resilient, and sharp recoveries can follow even the most severe downturns.

PART 5: BUILDING A PORTFOLIO

CHAPTER 21: THE ROLE OF TECHNOLOGY IN INVESTING

Technology has transformed nearly every aspect of investing, from how trades are executed to how portfolios are managed. In this chapter, we will explore how **fintech**, **AI**, and other innovations like **robo-advisors** and **algorithmic trading** are reshaping the investment landscape.

1. How Fintech is Changing the Investment Landscape

Fintech, short for financial technology, encompasses a wide range of tools and platforms that make investing more accessible, efficient, and cost-effective.

- **Online brokerages**: Platforms like **Robinhood**, **E*TRADE**, and others have democratized investing, allowing individual investors to trade stocks, bonds, and ETFs with minimal fees.
- **Investment apps**: Apps like **Acorns** and **Stash** enable users to automate their investments by rounding up purchases and investing spare change into diversified portfolios.
- **Fractional shares**: Investors can now purchase **fractional shares** of expensive stocks like Amazon or Google, making it easier for smaller investors to diversify.

2. AI and Algorithmic Trading

Artificial Intelligence (AI) and **machine learning** are playing an increasingly important role in analyzing vast amounts of market data to identify investment opportunities and optimize trading strategies.

- **Algorithmic trading**: Also known as **algo-trading**, this involves using computer algorithms to execute trades based on predefined criteria like price, volume, or time. This approach allows for faster, more efficient trades and can reduce human error.
- **AI-driven analysis**: AI can process massive amounts of data, including earnings reports, news articles, and social media sentiment, to provide insights that would be impossible for a human to analyze alone.

Strategy: While these tools offer powerful advantages, it's essential to understand their limitations and the risks of relying solely on technology for investment decisions.

3. Robo-Advisors

Robo-advisors use algorithms to manage portfolios based on an investor's goals, risk tolerance, and time horizon. They offer a low-cost, hands-off way to invest, making them popular with new and cost-conscious investors.

Popular robo-advisors include:

- **Betterment**
- **Wealthfront**
- **Vanguard Personal Advisor Services**

Benefits:

- **Low fees**: Robo-advisors typically charge lower fees than traditional financial advisors.
- **Automatic rebalancing**: Robo-advisors adjust your portfolio as needed to maintain your desired asset allocation.

Risks:

- **Limited personalization**: While robo-advisors are efficient, they may not offer the same level of personalized advice as human financial advisors.

CHAPTER 22: CASE STUDIES OF SUCCESSFUL INVESTORS

Some of the world's most successful investors have demonstrated timeless principles of investing. In this chapter, we'll explore the **key strategies** of renowned investors like **Warren Buffett**, **Ray Dalio**, and others, and draw **lessons** from their historic successes.

1. Warren Buffett: Value Investing Mastery

Warren Buffett, often referred to as the "Oracle of Omaha," is known for his **value investing** philosophy—buying stocks that are undervalued relative to their intrinsic worth and holding them for the long term.

Key Strategies:

- **Focus on fundamentals**: Buffett looks for companies with strong earnings, a competitive edge, and solid management.
- **Patience**: He believes in buying high-quality companies and holding them indefinitely, regardless of short-term market fluctuations.
- **Avoid speculation**: Buffett avoids chasing speculative investments, preferring businesses with proven track records.

Lesson: Focus on the long-term value of a company, not short-term market movements. Patience and discipline are critical to success.

2. Ray Dalio: Risk Parity and Diversification

Ray Dalio, founder of **Bridgewater Associates**, is known for his **risk-parity** strategy, which emphasizes balancing risk across various asset classes to achieve diversification.

Key Strategies:

- **All-weather portfolio**: Dalio's all-weather approach seeks to perform well in any economic environment by diversifying across stocks, bonds, commodities, and other assets.
- **Risk management**: Dalio stresses the importance of managing downside risk, ensuring that no single investment dominates the portfolio.

Lesson: Diversification and risk management are essential to weathering market volatility and achieving consistent returns.

3. John Bogle: Index Fund Pioneer

John Bogle, founder of **Vanguard Group**, revolutionized investing by creating the first **index fund**, which tracks the performance of a broad market index, like the S&P 500.

Key Strategies:

- **Low-cost investing**: Bogle emphasized the importance of minimizing fees, which can significantly erode long-term returns.
- **Market efficiency**: He believed that trying to beat the market was futile for most investors and that the best approach was to invest in a diversified, low-cost index fund.

Lesson: Keep costs low and invest in broad market indexes to capture long-term market growth without the need for constant trading.

Conclusion: Learning from the Best

Each of these investors has unique approaches to the market, but all share common themes: focus on fundamentals, discipline, diversification, and patience. By applying these timeless principles, you can improve your chances of achieving long-term investment success.

CHAPTER 23: ESTATE PLANNING AND WEALTH PRESERVATION

Effective **estate planning** ensures that your wealth is transferred according to your wishes and in the most tax-efficient manner possible. This chapter covers essential strategies such as **trusts, wills**, and **inheritance planning**, along with tips for tax-efficient wealth transfer.

1. Trusts, Wills, and Inheritance Strategies

- **Wills**: A will is a legal document that outlines how your assets will be distributed upon your death. It is the cornerstone of any estate plan and ensures that your assets are transferred to your heirs as you wish.
- **Trusts**: Trusts offer more control over how your assets are managed and distributed. There are various types of trusts, such as **revocable** and **irrevocable** trusts, each with its advantages. Trusts can help avoid probate, reduce estate taxes, and protect assets from creditors.
- **Beneficiary designations**: Ensure that your beneficiaries are up-to-date on your retirement accounts, life insurance policies, and other assets, as these typically override the instructions in your will.

2. Tax-Efficient Wealth Transfer

- **Gifting**: You can gift assets to your heirs during your lifetime to reduce the size of your taxable estate. Each year, you can give up to a certain amount per individual without incurring gift tax (consult current tax laws for specific limits).
- **Charitable giving**: Donating assets to charities can reduce your taxable estate and provide potential income tax deductions.
- **Generation-skipping transfer tax (GSTT)**: This tax applies to transfers made to individuals who are two or more generations younger than you (e.g., grandchildren). Proper planning can help minimize or avoid GSTT.

PART 6: SPECIAL CONSIDERATIONS

CHAPTER 24: SOCIALLY RESPONSIBLE INVESTING

Investors today are increasingly interested in aligning their investments with their values. **Socially Responsible Investing (SRI)** involves selecting investments based on **Environmental, Social, and Governance (ESG)** criteria. This chapter explores how to balance ethical considerations with potential returns.

1. Understanding ESG Criteria

- **Environmental**: Evaluating a company's impact on the environment, including its carbon footprint, waste management, and use of renewable resources.
- **Social**: Assessing how a company treats its employees, customers, and communities, including labor practices, diversity, and community engagement.
- **Governance**: Examining a company's leadership structure, transparency, and ethical behavior, including board diversity, executive compensation, and shareholder rights.

2. Balancing Ethics with Returns

- **Screening methods**: Investors can use **positive screening** (selecting companies with high ESG ratings) or **negative screening** (excluding companies with poor ESG practices).

- **Performance**: Studies have shown that ESG-focused investments can perform as well as, if not better than, traditional investments. However, careful research is necessary to ensure you're investing in companies that truly align with your values.

CHAPTER 25: THE IMPACT OF TAXES

Taxes can significantly impact your investment returns. This chapter covers how to invest in a tax-efficient manner and explains key concepts such as **capital gains**, **dividends**, and **tax-loss harvesting**.

1. Tax-Efficient Investing Strategies

- **Tax-advantaged accounts**: Maximize contributions to **401(k)s**, **IRAs**, and **Roth IRAs**, which offer tax benefits for retirement savings.
- **Tax-efficient funds**: **Index funds** and **ETFs** tend to be more tax-efficient than actively managed mutual funds because they have lower turnover and, thus, fewer taxable events.

2. Capital Gains, Dividends, and Tax-Loss Harvesting

- **Capital gains**: Long-term capital gains (for assets held over a year) are taxed at a lower rate than short-term gains. Consider holding investments longer to take advantage of these rates.
- **Tax-loss harvesting**: Offset gains by selling investments at a loss to reduce your taxable income. This strategy can help lower your tax bill and improve after-tax returns.

CHAPTER 26: GLOBAL INVESTING

Investing in international markets can offer diversification and growth opportunities. However, it also involves unique challenges, such as **emerging markets risks** and **foreign exchange fluctuations**.

1. Emerging Markets and Foreign Exchange Risks

- **Emerging markets**: These economies offer high growth potential but come with greater risks, such as political instability, regulatory changes, and currency volatility.
- **Currency risk**: Changes in foreign exchange rates can impact the value of your international investments. Consider hedging strategies or investing in funds that manage currency exposure.

2. International Diversification Benefits

Investing globally can reduce your portfolio's risk by spreading investments across different markets and economies. This diversification can help cushion against downturns in any single market.

PART 7: ADVANCED TOPICS

CHAPTER 27: BEHAVIORAL FINANCE

Human psychology often impacts investment decisions, sometimes leading to **irrational behavior** and **emotional pitfalls**. Understanding behavioral finance can help investors make more rational decisions.

1. How Psychology Impacts Financial Decisions

- **Overconfidence**: Many investors overestimate their ability to pick winning stocks, leading to excessive trading and potential losses.
- **Loss aversion**: The pain of losing is often felt more acutely than the pleasure of gaining. This bias can lead to poor investment decisions, such as selling winning investments too early or holding onto losing ones for too long.

2. Debunking Common Myths

- **"Timing the market"**: Many investors believe they can consistently predict market movements, but this is extremely difficult. A better approach is to focus on long-term investing and avoid trying to time the market.

CHAPTER 28: THE ROLE OF TECHNOLOGY IN MODERN INVESTING

Technology has revolutionized how we invest. From **robo-advisors** to **AI-driven analysis**, modern tools have made investing more accessible and efficient.

1. Robo-Advisors and AI in Investing

- **Robo-advisors**: These platforms use algorithms to manage portfolios, providing a low-cost and automated investment solution.
- **AI-driven analysis**: AI can process vast amounts of data to identify investment opportunities, offering sophisticated insights that were previously unavailable to retail investors.

2. The Impact of Fintech

Fintech companies are disrupting traditional financial services, offering new ways to **invest**, **analyze markets**, and **manage portfolios**. Staying informed about these trends can give investors an edge in today's rapidly evolving landscape.

CHAPTER 29: UNDERSTANDING MARKET CYCLES

The market moves in cycles, with periods of **boom** and **bust**. Understanding these cycles helps investors position their portfolios for long-term success.

1. Boom and Bust Cycles

- **Boom cycles**: Characterized by strong economic growth, rising stock prices, and investor optimism. These periods often precede corrections or crashes.
- **Bust cycles**: During downturns, economic activity slows, stock prices fall, and investor sentiment turns negative. These can provide buying opportunities for patient investors.

2. Predicting Market Movements

While predicting exact market movements is difficult, investors can look at **economic indicators**, such as interest rates, inflation, and corporate earnings, to gauge market conditions. However, long-term strategies like dollar-cost averaging can reduce the need to time the market.

CHAPTER 30: INVESTMENT ANALYSIS TOOLS

Investors rely on **fundamental** and **technical analysis** to make informed decisions. This chapter introduces key tools for both methods.

1. Fundamental and Technical Analysis Tools

- **Fundamental analysis**: Involves evaluating a company's financial health through metrics like **price-to-earnings (P/E) ratio**, **earnings per share (EPS)**, and **revenue growth**. This method helps identify undervalued stocks.
- **Technical analysis**: Focuses on price patterns and market trends using charts and technical indicators like **moving averages** and **Relative Strength Index (RSI)**.

2. Building Models for Valuation

Financial models such as **Discounted Cash Flow (DCF)** and **Price/Earnings-to-Growth (PEG)** help determine a company's intrinsic value, guiding investors toward decisions based on underlying financials rather than market sentiment.

PART 8: CASE STUDIES AND REAL-WORLD APPLICATIONS

CHAPTER 31: THE WARREN BUFFETT WAY

Warren Buffett, one of the world's most successful investors, follows principles of **value investing**. This chapter explores his strategies and lessons from his leadership of **Berkshire Hathaway**.

1. A Deep Dive into Buffett's Strategies

- **Value investing**: Buffett focuses on buying undervalued companies with strong fundamentals and holding them for the long term.
- **Patience and discipline**: Buffett is known for his patience, avoiding short-term speculation and waiting for the right opportunities.

2. Lessons from Berkshire Hathaway

Buffett's success comes from his careful selection of companies, his long-term outlook, and his ability to avoid emotional decision-making during market volatility. His strategy emphasizes **simplicity** and **fundamental analysis**.

CHAPTER 32: THE DOT-COM BUBBLE

The late 1990s saw a speculative bubble in technology stocks, followed by a sharp crash. This chapter explores what led to the **Dot-Com Bubble** and what investors can learn from it.

1. Lessons from the Late 1990s Tech Boom and Bust

- **Overvaluation**: Many tech companies were valued at prices far exceeding their actual earnings potential, driven by investor euphoria and market speculation.
- **Irrational exuberance**: Investors ignored fundamentals, leading to unsustainable valuations. When reality caught up, the bubble burst, causing widespread losses.

2. Managing Risk in Growth Stocks

Investors can learn from this event by focusing on companies with solid earnings and growth prospects, rather than speculative stocks. Diversification and valuation discipline are key to avoiding such pitfalls.

CHAPTER 33: THE 2008 FINANCIAL CRISIS

The **2008 financial crisis** was a watershed moment in modern investing. Understanding the causes and consequences of this crisis helps investors avoid similar mistakes.

1. Causes and Consequences of the Crisis

- **Subprime mortgages**: The crisis was triggered by risky lending practices in the housing market, leading to widespread mortgage defaults and a collapse in the financial system.
- **Global recession**: The fallout affected economies worldwide, leading to job losses, declining markets, and government bailouts.

2. Investment Strategies Post-Crisis

The aftermath of the 2008 crisis emphasized the importance of risk management, diversification, and avoiding over-leveraging. Investors who focused on **safe-haven assets** and **long-term stability** fared better during the downturn.

CHAPTER 34: CASE STUDY OF TESLA'S STOCK RISE

Tesla's meteoric rise in the 2010s offers insights into investing in **high-growth technology companies**. This chapter dissects what drove Tesla's stock and the associated risks.

1. Factors that Drove the Growth

- **Innovation and leadership**: Tesla's success is attributed to its focus on cutting-edge technology in electric vehicles, renewable energy, and the vision of CEO Elon Musk.
- **Market demand**: A growing market for electric vehicles and renewable energy pushed investor sentiment and stock price.

2. Risks of Investing in High-Growth Tech Companies

Investing in companies like Tesla carries risks due to **volatility**, **high valuations**, and **market expectations**. While high-growth stocks can offer large returns, they also come with significant downside risks if growth expectations are not met.

PART 9: FUTURE OF INVESTING

CHAPTER 35: THE ROLE OF AI AND BIG DATA

Artificial Intelligence (AI) and Big Data are transforming the investment landscape, offering powerful tools for analysis, decision-making, and predictive modeling.

1. How Machine Learning is Transforming Finance

AI can process vast amounts of data faster than humans, identifying patterns and trends that traditional methods might miss. Here are a few ways AI is reshaping finance:

- **Algorithmic trading**: AI-driven algorithms can execute trades in milliseconds, optimizing buy and sell decisions based on real-time data.
- **Robo-advisors**: AI is increasingly used in financial advisory services, automating investment management through algorithms based on a client's risk tolerance and financial goals. Robo-advisors offer cost-effective solutions for individual investors.
- **Credit scoring and risk management**: AI enhances credit risk assessment by analyzing diverse data points, improving the ability to predict defaults or market downturns.

2. Predictive Analytics in Investing

AI uses **predictive analytics** to forecast market movements by analyzing historical data and complex market variables. This technology offers investors enhanced decision-making tools:

- **Sentiment analysis**: By processing news, social media, and financial reports, AI can gauge market sentiment, helping investors anticipate market shifts.
- **Portfolio management**: AI can optimize portfolios by analyzing market conditions, rebalancing investments based on risk tolerance and performance metrics.

While AI promises efficiency and higher returns, investors must also be aware of its limitations, such as over-reliance on algorithms and lack of human intuition in unpredictable markets.

CHAPTER 36: SUSTAINABLE AND GREEN INVESTMENTS

Sustainable investing focuses on companies and assets that prioritize environmental, social, and governance (ESG) factors, reflecting a growing trend among investors who aim to align their portfolios with ethical values.

1. The Future of ESG Investing

ESG investing has gained momentum as climate change and social responsibility become more prominent global issues. Investors are increasingly directing capital towards companies with sustainable business practices, which may offer both ethical and financial benefits:

- **Environmental**: Companies focusing on renewable energy, sustainable agriculture, or waste reduction are more likely to succeed in a carbon-conscious world.
- **Social**: Firms that promote fair labor practices, diversity, and community engagement can build strong, ethical brands that attract consumers and investors alike.
- **Governance**: Corporations with transparent leadership and ethical governance structures are less prone to scandals, making them more stable investments in the long term.

2. Climate Change and its Impact on Investment Strategies

As governments and businesses prioritize reducing carbon

emissions, industries like **energy**, **transportation**, and **agriculture** will face significant disruptions. Investors can capitalize on these changes by:

- **Investing in green technology**: Renewable energy companies (e.g., solar, wind) are poised for long-term growth as the world transitions away from fossil fuels.
- **Avoiding high-risk industries**: Traditional energy companies, particularly those reliant on coal or oil, may experience increased regulatory pressures and declining demand.

Sustainable investing also enables investors to make a positive impact on the world while potentially benefiting from strong financial returns as the green economy grows.

CONCLUSION: ACHIEVING FINANCIAL INDEPENDENCE

Achieving financial independence means accumulating enough wealth to live without relying on earned income, allowing individuals the freedom to pursue their passions, retire comfortably, or weather unexpected financial challenges. This conclusion ties together key strategies discussed throughout the book.

1. Building Wealth Over Time

Wealth-building is a **long-term process**, where consistent investing, even in small amounts, can lead to significant growth over decades. Investors must focus on:

- **Compounding**: Reinvesting earnings to generate returns on returns, magnifying long-term growth.
- **Discipline**: Avoiding emotional reactions to short-term market fluctuations, and sticking to a well-structured investment plan.

By diversifying across asset classes and sectors, investors reduce their risk exposure and smooth out potential losses during volatile periods.

2. Balancing Risk and Reward

A key to successful investing is balancing **risk and reward**. The chapters on asset allocation and risk management have emphasized that:

- **Higher-risk investments** (e.g., stocks, cryptocurrencies) offer higher potential returns but come with volatility.
- **Lower-risk investments** (e.g., bonds, dividend stocks) offer stability and a predictable income stream but generally have lower returns.

Financial independence can be achieved by striking a balance between these two, ensuring that the portfolio grows while protecting it from major losses.

CHAPTER 37: CRAFTING YOUR LONG-TERM INVESTMENT PLAN

A long-term investment plan should be tailored to an investor's **financial goals**, **time horizon**, and **risk tolerance**. This chapter guides readers in structuring a personalized investment strategy that evolves as their needs change over time.

1. Defining Your Financial Goals

Investors must clearly define their goals, whether they're planning for **retirement**, buying a home, or achieving other financial milestones. These goals should be categorized as:

- **Short-term goals**: Less than five years (e.g., saving for a down payment on a house).
- **Medium-term goals**: 5-10 years (e.g., paying for a child's education).
- **Long-term goals**: 10+ years (e.g., retirement).

2. Setting a Strategy for Success

To craft a successful investment plan:

- **Determine risk tolerance**: Younger investors can generally take on more risk, while those nearing retirement might prefer a more conservative portfolio.
- **Diversify**: Spread investments across different asset classes

(stocks, bonds, real estate, etc.) to reduce risk.
- **Automate savings and investments**: Consistent contributions to an investment account, automated through salary deductions, help build wealth steadily.

Regularly reviewing and adjusting the plan as life circumstances change is crucial to maintaining progress toward financial independence.

CHAPTER 38: LESSONS FROM LEGENDARY INVESTORS

History's greatest investors, like **Warren Buffett**, **Peter Lynch**, and **Ray Dalio**, offer timeless lessons that all investors can apply. This chapter distills their key strategies into actionable insights.

1. Warren Buffett's Value Investing

Buffett's philosophy centers on investing in undervalued companies with solid fundamentals. His advice to the average investor is to:

- **Focus on the long term**: Buy companies you believe in and hold them indefinitely, ignoring short-term market noise.
- **Invest in what you understand**: Buffett emphasizes the importance of only investing in businesses you can comprehend. This reduces unnecessary risks and builds confidence in your investment choices.

2. Ray Dalio's All-Weather Portfolio

Dalio, founder of Bridgewater Associates, promotes the **All-Weather Portfolio**, which is designed to perform well in any economic condition. The portfolio is heavily diversified and balanced between different asset classes to reduce risk during downturns.

3. Peter Lynch's Growth Investing

Lynch made his fortune by identifying and investing in growth

companies. He advocates for individual investors to:
- **Do your homework**: Thorough research is critical in identifying companies with strong growth potential.
- **Stay patient**: Growth stocks can be volatile, but over the long term, companies that reinvest profits into expansion can generate substantial returns.

FINAL CONCLUSION: MASTERING THE ART OF INVESTING

Throughout this book, we have covered the fundamental principles and advanced strategies required to become a successful investor. From understanding how financial markets operate to learning how to build a diversified portfolio, each chapter has provided practical tools and insights to help readers navigate the complex world of investments.

Key Takeaways

1. **The Power of Knowledge**: The most successful investors aren't those who chase trends but those who build a solid foundation of knowledge. Whether it's learning about stocks, bonds, real estate, or cryptocurrencies, understanding the characteristics and risks of each asset class is critical to making informed decisions.
2. **Risk and Reward**: Every investment decision involves a balance between risk and reward. By diversifying your portfolio across different assets and markets, you can reduce risk while still capturing growth opportunities.
3. **The Role of Economic Indicators**: The performance of investments is often tied to broader economic trends like inflation, interest rates, and GDP. Understanding how these factors influence markets can help you anticipate shifts and protect your portfolio from downturns.

4. **The Importance of Strategy**: From value and growth investing to income-focused strategies, finding an approach that aligns with your goals, risk tolerance, and time horizon is essential. Strategies like index fund investing and value investing have been proven to build wealth over the long term, while newer trends such as ESG and sustainable investing align financial returns with ethical values.
5. **Psychology and Discipline**: Investing is not just a numbers game. It requires emotional discipline and the ability to stay rational during volatile times. Recognizing behavioral biases and avoiding emotional reactions can help prevent costly mistakes.
6. **Technology and the Future**: The rise of AI, big data, and fintech is transforming how we invest. These advancements offer powerful tools to manage risk, analyze markets, and automate portfolios, giving individual investors access to sophisticated strategies once reserved for professionals.
7. **The Long-Term Perspective**: Achieving financial independence is a marathon, not a sprint. Whether you are investing for retirement, wealth preservation, or future goals, having a long-term mindset allows you to weather market volatility and capitalize on the power of compounding.

Building Your Own Path to Financial Success

This book provides a roadmap for investors at all stages, from beginners learning the basics to seasoned investors looking to refine their strategies. The ultimate goal is to equip you with the tools to build a personalized investment plan that aligns with your unique financial goals.

By understanding the full spectrum of asset classes, mastering key strategies, and maintaining a disciplined, long-term approach, you can confidently navigate the evolving landscape of finance and investing.

FINAL WORDS

Successful investing is about making informed, disciplined choices, adapting to changing markets, and staying committed to long-term goals. As you move forward on your investment journey, remember that the best investors are always learning, adapting, and growing. Let the knowledge gained from this book serve as your foundation as you build wealth and achieve financial freedom.

www.ingramcontent.com/pod-product-compliance
Lightning Source LLC
Chambersburg PA
CBHW050302230526
45471CB00005B/1974